An Introduction to African Philosophy

Samuel Oluoch Imbo

ROWMAN & LITTLEFIELD PUBLISHERS, INC.
Lanham ▣ Boulder ▣ New York ▣ Oxford

ROWMAN & LITTLEFIELD PUBLISHERS, INC.

Published in the United States of America
by Rowman & Littlefield Publishers, Inc.
4720 Boston Way, Lanham, Maryland 20706

12 Hid's Copse Road
Cumnor Hill, Oxford OX2 9JJ, England

British Library Cataloguing in Publication Information Available

Library of Congress Cataloging-in-Publication Data
Imbo, Samuel Oluoch, 1961–
    An introduction to African philosophy / Samuel Oluoch Imbo.
      p.   cm.
    Includes bibliographical references and index.
    ISBN 0-8476-8840-2 (alk. paper). — ISBN 0-8476-8841-0 (pbk. :
alk. paper)
    1. Philosophy, African.   I. Title.
    B5305.I43   1998
    199'.6—dc21   97-48810
                                              CIP

ISBN 0-8476-8840-2 (cloth : alk. paper)
ISBN 0-8476-8841-0 (pbk. : alk. paper)

Printed in the United States of America

♾ ™ The paper used in this publication meets the minimum requirements of
American National Standard for Information Sciences—Permanence of Paper
for Printed Library Materials, ANSI Z39.48–1984.

To Yu-jung

Contents

Acknowledgments

I owe a huge debt of gratitude to many people who have contributed to this book over the years. First, my teachers, especially the late Henry Odera Oruka, who together with Dismas Masolo introduced me to comparative philosophy. Next, my students at Purdue University Calumet and at Hamline University, who unfailingly asked the crucial questions that challenged me to clarify my positions on the topics discussed here.

I am very grateful to Jeffrey Crawford, whose extensive comments on the manuscript at various stages were extremely useful. His suggestions, even those I did not agree with, made the book clearer than it might otherwise have been. Emmanuel Eze and Bill Lawson provided additional constructive guidance that made me revisit some previously unclear arguments.

My institution, Hamline University, provided a most supportive environment in which to finish writing this book. I particularly want to acknowledge the debt to my colleagues in the philosophy department, Duane Cady, Nancy Holland, and Stephen Kellert, for listening and providing opportunities for ongoing dialogue on these topics. Support from the College of Liberal Arts came in the form of the Hanna Grant, which freed me from material concerns during the summer of 1997.

Finally, my wife, Yu-jung Hu, to whom this book is dedicated. She was the first reader of every chapter and also typed and computer edited the manuscript through all its stages. Without her love, inspiration, and encouragement, this book would not have been completed.

Introduction

Much contemporary writing on African philosophy is a direct challenge to the bases and content of Western scholarship. Other writing that celebrates indigenous traditions is an indirect challenge to the view that in the absence of "great" written texts, traditional Africa could not claim to have had intellectual cultures. Indeed, the theme of whether philosophy can exist and thrive in the absence of written texts runs through many contemporary discussions in African philosophy.

A number of books, mostly anthologies, bring together articles from a wide range of academic journals where these debates on the nature and definition of African philosophy have been raging. Large parts of these anthologies are taken up with discussions of whether an African philosophy exists, how it is to be defined, what distinguishes it from Western philosophy, whether it is oral or written, and whether it can be accessible to non-Africans or is so unique that only Africans can understand it. Participants in the debates bring different definitions and underlying assumptions about what philosophy is, and it is therefore not surprising that African philosophy gets defined and classified in such different ways. Two general trends are discernible in the introductory texts. On the one hand, there is an ethnophilosophy that takes a culture-specific view of philosophy and finds African philosophy in the proverbs, myths, folk tales, sculptures, and traditional cultures. Opposed to ethnophilosophy is the universalist approach, which rejects culture-specific philosophy. Universalists for the most part are skeptical about the existence of a philosophy that is not written down and—if such a philosophy did come into existence—its ability to develop a tradition of debate and sustained inquiry. Within the universalist approach there is a minority, represented by Kenyan philosopher Henry Odera Oruka, that defends an oral philosophical tradition. Odera Oruka develops a thesis he calls *Sagacity*, according to which there were in traditional Africa sages who were philosophic in the strictest sense despite their illiteracy. He offers Socrates as a parallel example of a sage, who never wrote down his thoughts and yet is generally considered a great philosopher. The larger argument between the ethnophilosophers and universalists is really whether the notion of text should be restricted to its usual domain—the written word.

Despite the useful function of synthesizing arguments from diverse sources, the current literature almost invariably lacks variety in the number of topics represented and so serves as an introduction to African philosophy in only a limited sense. One such introductory text is Tsenay Serequeberhan's *African Philosophy: The Essential Readings*.[1] Even though he brings together some of the main voices of contemporary African philosophy, Serequeberhan limits the contributions in that collection to the writings of Africans. While it is important, in his words, to "hearken to what Africans have to say for themselves," the issue of whether non-Africans can contribute to African philosophy should itself be part of the ongoing discussion. Limiting the contributions to only those of Africans effectively sidesteps this larger debate. The anthology is also limited in another sense. Most of the articles confine themselves to the single issue of whether there exists such a thing as African philosophy. The book is thus imbalanced in the sense that most of the chapters dwell on questions of definition and justification. Such an introduction does not give an adequate indication of the landscape of African debates on metaphysics, epistemology, ethics, and aesthetics.

Another example of an anthology that has served as a vehicle for these debates on the nature and definition of African philosophy is Richard Wright's *African Philosophy: An Introduction*,[2] which first came out twenty years ago. The most often cited third edition was published in 1984. This anthology, like Serequeberhan's, suffers from an imbalance. In this case, the problem comes from leaning too heavily in the ethnophilosophical direction. As Kwame Anthony Appiah, a towering figure in contemporary African scholarship, has noted: "The only paper in Wright's collection that exemplifies the critical analysis that characterizes the best philosophy—the only paper that seems to me to offer a standard for African philosophy to aim at—is Kwasi Wiredu's 'How Not to Compare African Thought with Western Thought.' "[3] I take a slightly more charitable view than Appiah's in holding that with the possible exception of one or two, the rest of the essays, Wright's collection, by uncritically falling back on traditional cultures as acceptable materials for philosophical study, does not rise above the level of ethnophilosophy.

A book like M. Akin Makinde's *African Philosophy, Culture, and Traditional Medicine*[4] is not intended as an introduction to African philosophy, and it would be unfair to treat it as such. Yet insofar as it bears the title "African Philosophy," I highlight it because it illustrates a problem of a different kind. It purports to sidestep the whole debate about whether an African philosophy exists. Although the device of finding African philosophy "by means of some African traditional thinking which addresses itself to much the same philosophical issues as Western philosophy"[5] may lull Makinde into thinking that the question of the existence of African philosophy has successfully been ducked, this stratagem is in fact the uncritical embrace of one view of philosophy without regard to the implications of that view and without an examination of the alternatives. The product may indeed be insightful about traditional African medicine and its practice, but its status as philosophy must remain doubtful.

Recently Safro Kwame has anthologized Akan philosophy in *Readings in African Philosophy: An Akan Collection*.[6] Safro Kwame's work is similar in spirit to the work of another Akan philosopher, Kwame Gyekye,[7] whose focus is also on the Akan ethnic group. Although impressive in terms of breadth of topics covered (there are selections on traditional and current trends, metaphysics, epistemology, business ethics, and feminism), the anthology has a focus on only one ethnic group—the Akan group, composed of speakers of languages such as Twi, Fanti, Asante, and Akwapim in modern Ghana. The title "African Philosophy" is therefore overly ambitious—unless one holds a unanimist view of Africans whereby what is true of one ethnic group is also true of others.

There has been lately another group of books that I believe provide better introductions to African philosophy. One is an anthology by Albert Mosley entitled *African Philosophy: Selected Readings*.[8] Mosley brings together "texts by Africans, African-Americans, Europeans, and European-Americans." An advantage of this breadth in terms of contributors is that it places the problematics of an African philosophy in the broader context of the history of ideas. In the contributions by Africans and African Americans there is evident a construction by Europe of black people as fundamentally inferior and lacking in humanity. Here the problematic of "black consciousness" and "Pan-Africanism" is raised. Unfortunately, the confines of an anthology do not allow the exploration of these ideas and their implications in satisfactory detail. This is, however, a book that challenges the divisions of a people who have shared enslavement and denigration simply along color and national lines. The attempt to borrow from the African experience to understand the African American experience in America, or vice versa, however, is fraught with conceptual dangers. Some attempts to force a cultural or racial identity between Africans and African Americans simply rest on facile categorizations and an essentialism that requires more than an anthology to unpack.

Another excellent introduction is D. A. Masolo's *African Philosophy in Search of Identity.*[9] Masolo offers an impressive and comprehensive history of the last forty years of debates in African philosophy. In his expansive coverage of the panorama of African discourse, Masolo draws the reader into the core issues of concern to contemporary Africans while at the same time making connections between Anglophone and Francophone Africa and also between Africa and the rest of the world.

The foregoing books obviously leave room for more anthologies or monographs that are not limited in the variety of topics covered or in their historical breadth, but would also accurately represent the contemporary work in African philosophy. Parker English and Kibujjo M. Kalumba have recently supplemented the existing body of work in African philosophy with their title *African Philosophy: A Classical Approach.*[10] In their preface, the editors describe the text as containing "the classics, the written works which are most often cited by those who write African philosophy."[11] This is just one of the good things about the book. Its other merits include bringing together classics that are often no longer in print, while at the same time maintaining variety.

In 1997, three books edited by Emmanuel Chukwudi Eze were published, adding to the pool of texts in African philosophy. Two of these books, *African Philosophy: An Anthology*[12] and *Postcolonial African Philosophy: A Critical Reader,*[13] are excellent anthologies that contain essays ranging from those that define African philosophy to those that examine issues of ethics, knowledge and science, religion, art, race, and gender. Not only do Eze's anthologies represent diverse cultural and ideological perspectives, they make the transatlantic connections between Africans and African Americans—connections which are also a central concern of this book. Eze's third anthology, *Race and the Enlightenment: A Reader,*[14] is not directly about African philosophy. The essays in this collection represent the racist views of Europe's Age of Reason, and therefore indirectly raise the issue of what the systematic relationship between philosophy and race portends for the objectivity of philosophy as a discipline.

The present book aspires to the Masolo tradition of looking at African philosophy with a comparativist's eye. Rather than aiming for an expansive sweep, the focus is here on five questions that, if properly understood, introduce the reader not only to African philosophy but also to the wider project of philosophy. Currently debates on the nature and definition of African philosophy are scattered in a wide range of academic journals and anthologies. In that form it is a daunting task to follow the threads of the different arguments coherently. A lot of the discussion on African philosophy already takes place on the African continent where unfortunately, because of the expense and difficulty of publishing, that discussion usually remains confined. This book makes connections between the ideas spread out in the journals and anthologies. There are extensive quotations from the major discussants, allowing them to speak in their own voices while the narrative of the author connects these different voices. The use of extensive quotes woven into a simple narrative allows the advantages of an anthology as well as those of a monograph.

I have tried to keep out of the debates as much as possible, but I am sure the reader will detect where my sympathies lie. The main writings on African philosophy are divided here into three sections. The first addresses those perennial questions about the existence and definition of African philosophy. Debates on the nature, definition, and justification of African philosophy are grouped under the question, How is African philosophy to be defined? The second section deals with ethnophilosophy and its implications. There are two questions that get to the heart of the philosophical problems at hand. These questions are: Is ethnophilosophy really philosophy? and Is African philosophy unique? The last section makes connections that place African philosophy in a global context. In a world that has become a global village, questions about which language(s) should be used can no longer be ignored. Yet African philosophers continue to appear oblivious to the implications of the languages they choose for their craft. A connection with African American culture and literature is rarely made in other introductory texts (as the recent texts by Masolo and Mosley do). Even rarer are connections between African philosophy and feminism. The two questions that address these linkages are: What should be the language(s) of African philosophy? and Are there connections among African, African American, and feminist philosophies?

This format introduces the reader both to the specific discussions in African philosophy and to a comparativist outlook that seeks the broader implications of connections among African, African American and feminist philosophies for the discipline of philosophy and for related disciplines. These have always been my concerns as an African scholar. In my experience teaching African philosophy at the introductory level, my American students have often given the impression that the goings-on in Africa are unconnected to their experience. It is not surprising, then, that African philosophy would seem to them abstract and of merely academic interest. A manifestation of this sense of disconnectedness is the widespread feeling that in America, African philosophy should be of interest, if at all, only to African Americans—a feeling borne out by enrollment patterns in African philosophy classes offered in American universities. The question and discussion method adopted in this book, by making connections with the issues of racism and sexism, should make clear the relevance of discussions of African philosophy in America (even for those persons not previously exposed to any of these discussions). By making these connections, this book should overcome the imbalances of previous introductory texts, while mapping out the landscape of contemporary African philosophy and anticipating the directions of future discourse.

Notes

1. Tsenay Serequeberhan, ed., *African Philosophy: The Essential Reading* (New York: Paragon House, 1991).

2. Richard Wright, ed., *African Philosophy: An Introduction* (Lanham, Md.: University Press of America, 1984).

3. Kwame Anthony Appiah, *In My Father's House: Africa in the Philosophy of Culture* (New York: Oxford University Press, 1992), 102.

4. M. Akin Makinde, *African Philosophy, Culture, and Traditional Medicine* (Athens: Ohio University Press, 1988).

5. Makinde, *African Philosophy, Culture, and Traditional Medicine*, 44.

6. Safro Kwame, ed., *Readings in African Philosophy: An Akan Collection* (New York: University Press of America, 1996).

7. Kwame Gyekye, *An Essay on African Philosophical Thought: The Akan Conceptual Scheme* (Cambridge: Cambridge University Press, 1987).

8. Albert Mosley, ed., *African Philosophy: Selected Readings* (Englewood Cliffs, N.J.: Prentice Hall, 1995).

9. D. A. Masolo, *African Philosophy in Search of Identity* (Bloomington: Indiana University Press, 1994).

10. Parker English and Kibujjo M. Kalumba, eds., *African Philosophy: A Classical Approach* (Englewood Cliffs, N.J.: Prentice Hall, 1996).

11. English and Kalumba, *African Philosophy*, xi.

12. Emmanuel Chukwudi Eze, ed., *African Philosophy: An Anthology* (Cambridge, Mass.: Blackwell, 1997).

13. Emmanuel Chukwudi Eze, ed., *Postcolonial African Philosophy: A Critical Reader* (Cambridge, Mass.: Blackwell, 1997).

14. Emmanuel Chukwudi Eze, ed., *Race and the Enlightenment: A Reader* (Cambridge, Mass.: Blackwell, 1997).

PART ONE

Definitions
of
African
Philosophy

◙

How Is

African Philosophy

to Be Defined?

◙

The common opinion among ordinary people is that philosophy is a difficult subject. Philosophers are thought to use strange and difficult words or, worse, to use ordinary words in strange and difficult ways. What exactly it is that philosophers do is not easy to pin down, but everyone knows that their subject has no practical applications. I begin with these common misconceptions to show why defining philosophy is bound to be a controversial enterprise. The attempt in this book will be doubly controversial since we seek to define not only philosophy, but African philosophy as well.

What Is Philosophy?
The difficulty of pinning down simple definitions of philosophy such as one would give of history, sociology, or anthropology can be explained by the richness and variety of what can be called philosophical. Philosophy begins with our everyday experiences of sleeping, waking up, eating and drinking, being in relationships with others, going to school, paying taxes, practicing religion, growing old, and dying. It is not these experiences that are themselves philosophical, since we know there are many people who go through life untroubled by, and impervious to, the problems they pose. Philosophy truly begins with the sense of wonder that pushes one to attempt to understand one's life and one's place in the universe. Owing to its complexity, the universe does not present itself

to all of us in the same manner. Our experiences, therefore, are made intelligible partly against the background of the culture and environment in which those experiences take place. Thus, part of the variety in philosophy is due to the variety of cultures and is evidence of the way philosophy takes on different intellectual bents as it is practiced in different places. This observation does not in any way entail the problematic claim made by earlier anthropologists that races, cultures, and even nations each have their own characteristic mentality. It is more accurate to point out that these categories of race, culture, and nationality (which are themselves problematic and stand in need of critical analysis) do not determine but rather influence the attitudes and methods adopted and the choice of questions asked. A philosophy always springs, however indirectly, from the society in which the philosopher grows up, with its religious proclivities or lack thereof, the social class from which the philosopher has been drawn, and the events that have shaped the philosopher's education.

Variety in philosophy arises out of the complexity of the universe in another way. Human experiences are rich and varied. The ordinary experiences enumerated here lead to philosophical questions of very different kinds. If one thinks about food, one can wonder what would be wrong, if anything, with buying and eating eight big meals a day. The experience of religion may make one wonder about what makes one's religion truer or better than that of a neighbor from a distant and exotic land. Similarly, the experience of paying taxes may lead those who live under a colonial government to question the justice of the whole arrangement. The terminal illness or the death of friends or relatives evokes reflection about the hereafter. Over time philosophers have grouped these questions and problems into different branches of philosophy—ethics, epistemology, metaphysics, logic, and social and political philosophy. Ethics deals with questions about right and wrong, duties and obligations, and questions about the good life. Since ethics also concerns itself with problems of values, some philosophers consider aesthetics (the philosophy of fine art) and the philosophy of religion to be closely related. Epistemology is the branch of philosophy concerned with theories of knowledge, opinions, and questions about how or whether we can be certain of anything in the quest for truth. Metaphysics, which some philosophers prefer to call ontology, groups together questions about the difference between reality and appearance and questions of things changing from one mode of existence to another. Logic is the branch that specializes in distinguishing valid forms of arguments from invalid ones, and sound reasoning from unsound. And since as human beings we must live around other people, social and political philosophy is the branch that helps us deal with questions about such things as the legitimacy of government, our obligations to the people around us, and how to design just laws.

All these branches of philosophy are so closely related because the problems and questions they address are themselves intertwined. It becomes obvious that the problems of philosophy are not divided into neat compartments, because a discussion of any question soon spills over into answering related questions. This would seem to suggest that the ultimate questions of philosophy are all equally important. The history of philosophy, however, shows that philosophers have not always agreed even on this seemingly simple point. The different branches have developed different methods for dealing with philosophical problems. This tempted some philosophers to see their own preferred branch of philosophy as the essence of the discipline. An early phase in the history of philosophy saw the reduction of philosophy to metaphysics. Logic, ethics, and epistemology were important only insofar as they contributed to an understanding of the totality of being. Centuries later the metaphysicians faced stiff opposition from a group that came to be known as logical positivists, who held that any proposition that could not be verified with natural facts was a pseudoproposition and therefore nonsense. On this reductionist view metaphysical propositions fail the tests of verifiability and linguistic analysis, both of which are the tests all meaningful philosophy must pass. In our time, the major challenge to mainstream philosophy is a trend called postmodernism. There is no simple way to define postmodernism. The most general characterization of postmodernism is that its emphasis is on calling into question the foundational concepts at the heart of Western philosophy. For instance, the idea of an atomic and rights-holding self, that is so crucial to Western philosophy and religion, is shown to be a myth. With the disappearance of the self, the systems of ethics and politics dependent on that idea come crumbling down. Postmodernism challenges the Western idea that there is one reality that is accessible to any impartial observer. Postmodern philosophers object to the Western philosophical tradition that grew out of Plato and Aristotle because that tradition assumed foundations or fundamentals that were universal to all human experience. Postmodernists have argued that the traditional approaches in Western philosophy systematically exclude and marginalize some stories and experiences. Postmodern philosophy therefore deconstructs the Greek *philos* (love) and *sophia* (wisdom) in a way that does not allow any one philosophy to reign supreme. The usual way of implicitly claiming superiority is, for example, by claiming or implying that non-Western intellectual contributions could not be original but had to be borrowed from Greece. This, as we shall see, is an approach to philosophy vigorously opposed by many Africans. Post-modernists call rather for an inclusive approach that allows the different experiences of humanity to construct complementary narratives.

The coming and going of these movements within philosophy shows us clearly that no philosophical school ever captures the truth once and for all. Another school always comes up to correct oversights and blind spots, to revise erroneous observations and conclusions, and to elaborate on insights previously offered as timeless. The history of philosophy shows that when a philosopher constructs a theory to explain some social or natural fact, it will not be long before alternative theories are offered that question its assumptions. Attempting to explain things can lead to new ways of looking at and thinking about old problems. Philosophers are therefore original in the sense of taking fresh approaches to recurring problems. False starts and a regress of explanations thus contribute to overall advances and progress.

Clearly, then, there is no one philosophical school or method that is always dominant, completely confident in its conclusions. There is simply no single method of dealing with philosophical problems. Some philosophers are analytic, concentrating on careful analysis of ordinary speech to discover therein pseudoproblems caused by faulty language usage. Other philosophers are prescriptive, believing that it is possible for people to influence one another's actions and emotions, and thus they outline ways in which people should act. Yet others are dialectical, always working their way into contradictions from which they attempt to glean new insights. Some philosophers adopt none of these methods. What philosophers share is an open-mindedness which allows for the digging up of unacknowledged presuppositions, an openness that allows for the existence of competing and alternative explanations of possibilities, and a willingness to suspend judgment in the absence of evidence. Philosophy is thus best understood as a process rather than a fixed body of knowledge. The hope is that this process will yield a tentative body of knowledge that embodies principles and judgments based on knowledge of social and material reality available at the time. This body of knowledge is itself under constant interpretation and analysis. Philosophical method is universal. The problems which philosophy addresses will, of course, be colored by specific historical, cultural, and geographical particularities. Philosophy in its varied manifestations must exhibit the following characteristics:

- Open-mindedness (willingness to afford a fair hearing to all)
- Skepticism (of received opinions and the status quo)
- A systematic approach (showing connections between different parts of belief/thought systems)
- A basis in justifying reasons (to convince informed, nonsectarian people)
- Universality (although its methods and questions remain the same, interpretations and applications will differ from place to place)

The foregoing discussion of philosophy is particularly relevant in the context of Africa. Africans today are challenging the treatment of their continent by the traditional disciplines. One can begin with the observation that the phrase "African philosophy" provokes a type and degree of debate that does not usually accompany formulations such as "Jewish philosophy," "American philosophy," or "European philosophy." One who is unfamiliar with Jewish, American, or European philosophy needs only to ask what that philosophy is; the existence of these philosophies is taken for granted. No calls for extended justifications of their existence are deemed necessary. The debate within African philosophy differs in the sense that the existence of the philosophy itself comes into question. Most of the early discussion in the field has thus been of a justificatory nature and has aimed primarily at laying the foundation and defining the parameters. Naturally, then, African philosophy appears to the newcomer to take a defensive posture. A scrutiny of that defensive posture, I believe, unlocks key insights into the peculiar position of African philosophy. It goes a long way in explaining why African philosophy has been made to appear unequal to other world philosophies. Exploring the meaning of African philosophy quickly brings to the fore the different conceptions of "philosophy," often held implicitly. Secondly, the political dimensions of the whole debate become inescapable. A careful analysis of the views of those skeptical about the existence of African philosophy serves the useful function of unearthing conceptions of philosophy that might otherwise remain at the level of implicit presuppositions. Three broad senses of African philosophy are discernible, which I have categorized as the ethnophilosophical, universalist, and hermeneutical approaches.

Ethnophilosophical Approaches

According to the group of poets, philosophers, and anthropologists collectively known by their detractors as ethnophilosophers, philosophy is
to be found embedded in the mythical, linguistic, and religious worldviews of the different cultures, and as such philosophy becomes unique
to its geographical applications. African philosophy, on this view, is
unique and consists of laying bare the belief systems and ethnological
concepts such as magic, language, personhood, time, and ethics. The
ethnophilosophical approach in African philosophy is best exhibited in
the writings of Placide Tempels, Leopold Sédar Senghor, and Alexis Kagame.

Placide Tempels on Bantu Philosophy

The consensus now is that publication of Tempels's *La Philosophie Bantoue* in 1945[1] was the spark that ignited the debate about African philosophy. For a long time the literature devoted to answering the question, Is
there an African philosophy? has continued to spring from, and respond
to, the work of Tempels. Tempels (1906–1977) was a Belgian missionary
who worked for many years among the Baluba (plural of Luba) people
who live in the lower Congo. The Baluba are an ethnic group that is
part of the larger Bantu family. By titling his book *Bantu Philosophy*,
Tempels obviously saw his work as applicable to the Bantu family of
ethnic groups as a whole, not just to the Baluba. No wonder the book
attracted so much attention. A catalyst for a broad range of responses,
Bantu Philosophy was a watershed in African philosophy, even if not for
the reasons the author intended. His report of a collective philosophy
among the Bantu of the lower Congo was effectively the birth of what
is today called ethnophilosophy. His "discovery" of Bantu philosophy
was intended to aid Western "educationists" in their "mission to civilize" the Africans.[2]

It is important to note that Tempels takes the view of philosophy as
the collective property of all the individuals of a culture. Their philosophy is their lived experience. Tempels extracts "Bantu philosophy" from
his observations of the behavior, customs, and language of the Luba
people of Central Africa. His method is therefore to extrapolate to the
Bantu and the African what he observes among the Baluba. Of his
method, he says:

> What is the best way in which to set out a systematic exposi-
> tion of Bantu philosophy while justifying the objectivity of

our hypothesis? . . . We could begin by a comparative study of the languages, modes of behavior, institutions and customs of the Bantu; we could analyze them and separate their fundamental ideas; finally we could construct from these elements a system of Bantu thought.

This, as a matter of fact, is the method that I followed myself.[3]

This method of generalization that Tempels adopted has come to haunt latter-day ethnophilosophers. Universalists like Hountondji have argued that just as it is foolhardy to hope to arrive at a people's philosophy via an exposition of their rituals and material culture, so too is it misguided to interpret Baluba worldviews as applicable to all Bantu people, or even Bantu worldviews as representative of all Africans.

Tempels is clear about the evidence at his disposal. The Bantu worldview is intricate and complex. The beliefs, myths, and cosmology of the Bantu are interwoven with their moral codes. In this mix one also finds a religious dimension of Bantu beliefs about ancestors, gods, and spirits; how the Bantu see the world and understand their place in it. Tempels's ethnophilosophy, by describing what he takes to be the Bantu worldview, treats philosophy as the expression of these collective values, often developed unconsciously in proverbs, riddles, stories, and songs. Everyday experiences and practices—even practices that do not specifically deal with thinking or reflection—are seen as embodying deep aspects of the culture's philosophy. For example, farming or merely going about day-to-day interactions are not specifically intellectual tasks. Yet they cannot be accomplished successfully without a deep (albeit intuitive) understanding of the culture's philosophy.

Bantu philosophy, for Tempels, can be reduced to the idea of vital force. In European philosophy, the concept is most recognizable in the French philosopher Henri Bergson's (1859–1941) élan vital. The concept of vital force as explained by Tempels therefore shows its Bergsonian roots. The basic premise in Bergson's intellectual system is a faith in direct intuition as an avenue for the attainment of knowledge. Intuition stands in direct opposition to the rationalism and scientific outlook of European philosophy. This force, the élan vital, has endured through time, moves all living things, and makes possible a superior kind of knowledge than that attained from the instinctual or intellectual faculties working separately. Tempels's discipleship to the theory of élan vital is obvious. He describes a Bantu ontology that differentiates between be-

ings in a hierarchy. Beings higher up in the hierarchy strengthen or
enfeeble those lower down. Although created by the highest force
(God), the hierarchy is anthropocentric because the created universe is
seen as centered around human forces. Forces are ranked in relation to
their ability to influence (positively or negatively) other forces. The
Bantu rank forces in the following descending order: God, spirits of the
ancestors, humans, animals, plants, and inanimate objects. Still, Tempels
understands:

> We need not expect the first African who comes along, espe-
> cially the young ones, to be able to give us a systematic expo-
> sition of his ontological system. None the less, this ontology
> exists; and it penetrates and informs all the thought of these
> primitives; it dominates and orientates all their behavior.[4]

What conclusion should we draw about Tempels's attempt to articulate Bantu philosophy based on his extended sojourn among the Baluba?
Is he presenting an authentic African philosophy—a discovery of something new and absent in the Western world? Are his descriptions too
tainted by Christian presuppositions and by his goal of "civilizing" the
Bantu to be considered a fair, unbiased, and adequate evaluation? Is it
possible to uncouple the explanatory value of the descriptions by Tempels from his Christian ideology?

Tempels devotes the book to presenting Bantu philosophy in the various aspects of its ontology, wisdom or criteriology, psychology, ethics,
and the overarching concept of vital force. Throughout the whole controversial book the Bantu do not formulate any of this philosophy themselves, for they are not reflective enough. They are too immersed in it.
In Tempels's view, each has subsumed his or her individuality to the
collective. There seems, however, a more important reason given by
Tempels as to why Bantu philosophy is articulated by him rather than
the Bantu themselves. The Bantu could not directly formulate their philosophy themselves because of the inadequacy of their vocabulary. Being
"non-civilized," Bantu languages are not equipped to capture the nu-
ances of what Tempels holds up as the standard for all philosophy—
Aristotelian and Thomistic thinking (this is not surprising when one
considers that Tempels was of the Franciscan tradition). There are passages in which Tempels is at pains to convey that he uses the terms "non-
civilized" and "primitive" descriptively and not in their derogatory
senses. The following passage is telling:

This "discovery" of Bantu philosophy is so disconcerting a revelation that we are tempted at first sight to believe that we are looking at a mirage. In fact, the universally accepted picture of primitive man, of the savage, of the proto-man living before the full blossoming of intelligence, vanishes beyond hope of recovery before this testimony. . . . We feel that we should speak "from one school of wisdom to another," "from one ideal to another," "from one conception of the world to another conception of it." The gods are dethroned, the disinherited stand before us as equals.[5]

A close reading of this passage reveals the meaning Tempels intended. The word "primitive" does not mean societies either earlier in time or inferior to other kinds. It is thus entirely possible that noncivilized societies, while being less developed than civilized societies in some respects, may nonetheless be more developed in other respects. If the Bantu cannot articulate her philosophy, it is because she does not need to. Her every activity embodies her philosophy. Tempels, who comes from a radically different society with a radically different conception of the world, considers himself much better placed to articulate Bantu philosophy. His civilized society is egocentric, emphasizes reflection, and conceives of the individual as atomic and autonomous. Consequently, the language of civilized societies is more developed and allows observers like Tempels to formulate ideas that in primitive cultures are only held implicitly. According to Tempels, the proof that complex ontological ideas are indeed held implicitly by the Bantu is that when he submitted his formulations of Bantu philosophy to the people themselves they agreed that he had correctly stated what they meant.

The work of Placide Tempels raises crucial philosophical questions that will be taken up in Chapter 2. The work of another ethnophilosopher, Leopold S. Senghor, raises these same questions.

Leopold Sédar Senghor on Negritude
The work of Senegalese statesman and man of letters Leopold S. Senghor (1906–)—the theory of negritude[6]—presents another variation on the theme of ethnophilosophy. Educated in both Dakar in Senegal and at the Sorbonne in Paris, Senghor was influenced by his contacts with Martinican Aimé Césaire and Guyanese Leon Damas. The alliance of these three led to the founding of the negritude movement in Paris. He was also influenced by the Harlem Renaissance through the work of

poet Langston Hughes and by the mood of Europe through interactions with his classmate and friend Georges Pompidou at l'Ecole normale su-perieure in Paris. Senghor posits for Africans, and indeed for all black people, a different way of apprehending the world from the European. The implications for philosophy are obvious. If Senghor is right, there must be a distinctively African epistemology with its own methodology for comprehending the universe. Senghor grounds his sociopolitical phi-losophy of negritude in the idea that the African experience of the world is based on emotion, not reason.

Negritude is a consciousness of the world through the medium of emotion, and the expression of emotion is at the center of African cul-ture. In contrast to Europeans, Senghor held, Africans in their languages, experiences, and cultures demonstrate a distinct mode of apprehension. He held that Africans were different from but not inferior to Europeans, and he led the negritude movement of philosophers, anthropologists, and poets in defending an unscientific, unanalytical, and untechnical Af-rican mind. Defending this intuitively odd proposition, Senghor says:

> Thus, I explain myself. However paradoxical it may seem, the vital force of the Negro African, his surrender to the ob-ject, is animated by reason. Let us understand each other clearly; it is not the *reasoning-eye* of Europe, it is the *reason of the touch*, better still, the *reasoning-embrace*, the sympathetic reason, more closely related to the Greek *logos* than to the Latin *ratio*. . . . At any rate, Negro-African speech does not mould the object into rigid categories and concepts without touching it; it polishes things and restores their original color, with their texture, sound and perfume; it perforates them with its luminous rays to reach the essential surreality in its innate humidity—it would be more accurate to speak of sub-reality. European reasoning is analytical, discursive by utiliza-tion; Negro-African reasoning is intuitive by participation.[7]

In this passage, Senghor explains his thesis that the Negro African inherits from his ancestors a consciousness of the world according to which the subject and object of observation, the natural and supernatu-ral, the mundane and divine, the material and the spiritual, are united in an inseparable oneness. This oneness is apprehended using the gift of emotion. Senghor's theory relies upon drawing attention to what he calls the Negro African practice of accommodation which is quite different from the obsessive concern with difference he sees everywhere in European thought. His project begins with a view of the Negro in universal terms. One of the tenets of negritude thus is the unity of Negro consciousness across all continents. Further, Senghor's theory of race rests on positing an intrinsic and qualitative difference between the European and the Negro African. This must be his meaning when he says:

> From our ancestors we have inherited our own method of knowledge. . . . In contrast to the classic European, the Negro African does not draw a line between himself and the object; he does not hold it at a distance, nor does he merely look at it and analyze it. After holding it at a distance, after scanning it without analyzing it, he takes it vibrant in his hands, careful not to kill or fix it.[8]

We have here, in principle, an acknowledgment of a distinctly African epistemology that is inherited. It has its own methodologies for evaluating natural or social phenomena. From their respective ancestors, the Europeans have inherited their reason and logic, while the Negro Africans have inherited soul and emotion. Unlike Eurocentric readings of these differences, however, Senghor formulates a theory that puts a positive value on both the European and Negro systems. Whereas ethnologists like Lucien Levy-Bruhl had seen in the prelogical and unanalytic mentality of the savage the proof of primitivity, Senghor maintains that each civilization and race has an "irreplaceable" truth. Instead of cultures, races, and civilizations denigrating each other, Senghor teaches that their uniqueness opens avenues for dialogue.

Now, the complexity of Senghor's thought can be explained partly by his membership and involved participation in the two worlds of Europe and Africa. On the one hand, his studies in France equipped him with an intimate knowledge of, and familiarity with, Continental philosophy. In 1983 Senghor was elected to the French Academy, which acknowledged him as one of the most important writers of the century and made him a guardian of the French language. Earlier, in 1949, he had been elected to the European Assembly in Strasbourg. On the other hand, he grew up in a largely traditional setting and was engaged throughout his life in Senegalese politics. During the 1930s and 1940s, Senghor and his friends Aimé Césaire of Martinique and Leon Damas of French Guyana had undertaken an exploration of black consciousness that they called negritude, with its political and artistic expressions and reassertion of African values. Senghor became active in politics in the 1940s and pursued a political path that led him to the presidency of the new republic of Senegal in 1960 (a post from which he voluntarily stepped down in 1981). Senghor's reassertion of the value of being black to his contemporary countrymen and countrywomen should be seen partly as a search for a political strategy, a methodology, that would work for Africans in their quest to reclaim their dignity and rightful place among other members of the human race. His work reflects an era during which African civilizations were being depreciated by colonialism. It was clear to him that European "methods of knowledge" were not equal to the task of comprehending the smell, touch, and feel—indeed the depth and richness—of African ways and values.

Those who have been charitable to Senghor admit that his strategy changed the way Europeans thought of Africa. His contribution was therefore to reassert the value of a continent that was almost entirely colonized and whose inhabitants were considered savages, barbarians, and sub-human. One such positive appraisal of Senghor's work is in a recent anthology by Parker English and Kibujjo Kalumba, wherein Parker English pronounces the theory of negritude "one of the most insightful and controversial themes in African philosophy."[9] His treatment of Senghor, though it is well balanced and takes into account the various criticisms of negritude, nevertheless remains positive in its appreciation of the complexity of Senghor's thought.

Senghor's detractors observe that the contradictions of his life have outweighed any valuable contributions. Even though he may have seen himself as making Europeans think more clearly about Africa, by essentially endorsing European definitions of Africa Senghor helped reinforce racist myths and neocolonialism. Ironically, by asserting emotion as an African value and reason as European, Senghor is accused of being a spokesman for Europe. More specifically, Senghor echoes a European author like Lucien Lévy-Bruhl who writes explicitly of the differences between the primitive African and the civilized Europeans. Senghor may also be seen as a spokesman for the other mainstream Western authors (Emmanuel Eze has given examples of primary texts from Immanuel Kant, Johann Gottfried von Herder, Thomas Jefferson, and Georg Wilhelm Friedrich Hegel in his book *Race and the Enlightenment: A Reader*) who, more subtly than Lévy-Bruhl, also associated rationality with Europe and barbarism and unreason with Africa. Further, critics point out a gap between his poetry and his politics. Senghor is known universally for his mind and love of humanity, as evidenced in the collection of his poetry called *Shadow Songs* (*Chants d'Ombre*, 1945), poems that include "Black Woman" (*Femme Noire*), "Black Mask" (*Masque Negre*), and "Ethiopiques," which praises being and thinking black. Yet in his career as president his actions were not consonant with his great poetry, and not once did he claim to be or act as a democrat. In the end, Senghor's contribution to philosophy and to African thought must be assessed in the context of his multifaceted roles as a complex man, poet, politician, president, and humanist.

Alexis Kagame on Linguistic Ethnophilosophy

A Catholic priest from Rwanda, Alexis Kagame (1919–1981) articulates a philosophy very similar to that of Tempels. While not agreeing entirely with Tempels, many Africans like Kagame have cheered the "discovery" of a unique and collective Bantu philosophy. Such a discovery was seen as serving important psychological needs of establishing or at least re-claiming a long-denied humanity. As Tempels had worked among the Baluba, Kagame worked among his Banyarwanda people. (The people of Rwanda are collectively called Banyarwanda. Their language is Kinya-rwanda.) Kagame's method was to study the Kinyarwanda language to elucidate a philosophy of being. By rooting his analysis in language, Kagame's attempt to reveal features of a Bantu worldview completes the picture started by Tempels. The primary linguistic concerns with syntax and semantics are important for Kagame in *Philosophie Bantou-Rwandaise de L'Etre* because he believes that people who speak the same language share abstract philosophical concepts. These abstract concepts are not held explicitly or consciously. They appear in proverbs, myths, legends, and social institutions. Thus for Kagame, as for Tempels, implicit onto-logical ideas provide the glue for the habits and values that are transmit-ted from one generation to another. The perennial social creation and transmission of values cannot take place in the absence of underlying philosophical concepts that are discernible in the structure of ordinary language. Thus, the importance of language for philosophy.

Kagame's main contribution is in the development of a theory of categories reminiscent of the systems of Plato, Aristotle, and Kant. In-deed it is important to note the Thomistic/Aristotelian roots of his ap-proach. St. Thomas Aquinas held that all beings are imbued with powers and faculties that proceed from their souls. In these powers or faculties there is a certain hierarchy. The higher the power, therefore, the wider and more comprehensive its object. In ascending order, then, there are inanimate objects, beings with a vegetative faculty, beings with a sensitive faculty, and beings with a rational faculty. God stands at the top of the hierarchy. Kagame's insight builds on something familiar to speakers of Bantu languages. Bantu languages are class languages, which means that words are divided into classes depending on whether, for example, they designate a living thing, a person, or an inanimate object. Kinyarwanda has eleven such word classes, each of which can be subsumed under four basic philosophical categories:

- Category of person: Words with the determinative *-mu-* in the singular and *-ba-* in the plural
- Category of things or objects: Words with the determinative *-ki-* in the singular and *-bi-* in the plural
- Category of place and time: Words with the determinative *-ha-*
- Category of mode: Words with the determinative *-ku-*

The categories are the most general types of being *-ntu-* and may therefore be summarized thus:

- *Umuntu* (human being)
- *Ikintu* (nonhuman being)
- *Ahantu* (place and time)
- *Ukuntu* (Aristotelian category of quantity)

God does not belong to any of the four categories.

Although Kagame does not quote Tempels, their fundamental ideas are similar, and the essential features of the latter's doctrines reappear regularly in Kagame. Being, in whatever category, belongs to that category because it possesses certain properties. Even though the categories are mutually exclusive, there can be interaction between them. *Umuntu*, the category imbued with intelligence, has a consciousness that allows it to use objects that do not possess the same capacity. Action is the actualization of a faculty. *Ikintu* does not have the capacity to actualize itself. This allows an *umuntu* to stand in respect to an *ikintu*, in the relation of possession, a relation in which the *ikintu* is at the disposal of the being that has intelligence. The traces of Tempels's vital force are all too clear in Kagame.

There is a disagreement between the two, however. Tempels maintained that every being had force—even though some beings have stronger force than others. Kagame, by elevating the standing of intelligence, is led to the position that only *umuntu* have real force. The foundation of Bantu philosophy for Kagame is therefore the *umuntu*, the existence endowed with intelligence. On that foundation must be built an understanding of the existence of different beings, the interaction between these beings, and the place of God in the Bantu world.

While Kagame's work has obviously been influenced by Tempels, a stronger influence is Kagame's scholastic background from which he imports categories to transplant in his own culture. As is to be expected, Kagame justifies his procedure using the Thomistic belief in the unity of rationality across human traditions and cultures. What should strike anyone seeking to penetrate his understanding of African philosophy is a procedure founded on a belief that Aristotelian and scholastic philosophies faithfully speak for all humanity. If it is good enough for the Aristotelian, it is good enough for Kagame. Bantu philosophy thus strangely conforms to the contours of Europe, Kagame's attempts to distance himself from Tempels notwithstanding.

Universalist Definitions of African Philosophy

Anyone who examines the literature cannot fail to be struck by the frequency of articles with such titles as "Is There an African Philosophy?";[10] "African Philosophy: Does It Exist?";[11] "Do We Have an African Philosophy?";[12] and "Is There an African Philosophy? The Politics of a Question."[13] These titles, which focus on questions about the existence of African philosophy, are revealing in two ways. In the first place, attempts to prove or disprove the existence of African philosophy quickly bring to light the different conceptions of "philosophy," often held implicitly, that people bring to the discussion. Secondly, the frequency of such titles is an indirect pointer that there is a great deal riding on the answer one gives concerning the existence of African philosophy and that this is not mere quibbling about semantics.

A careful analysis of the views of those skeptical about the existence of African philosophy and those who defend African philosophy in its different modes of existence serves the useful function of unearthing conceptions of philosophy that might otherwise remain at the level of implicit presuppositions. One of the broad senses in which African philosophy may be understood emerges best in the works of Kwasi Wiredu, Paulin Hountondji, Peter Bodunrin, and Henry Odera Oruka. These philosophers are not always comfortable about being grouped together. Although they may differ in the details, they all take a universalist outlook that begins with the definition of philosophy as an objective and universal enterprise. As such, philosophy is not culture dependent but is rather a systematic and methodological inquiry that should not be altered by its geographical applications. To develop what I take to be the universalist orientation in African philosophy, I will draw from the works of Kwasi Wiredu, Paulin Hountondji, and Henry Odera Oruka.

Kwasi Wiredu on Sifting Philosophy from Cultures

Kwame Anthony Appiah captures the universalist focus of fellow Ghanaian Kwasi Wiredu (1931–) thus: "For Wiredu there are no African truths, only truths—some of them about Africa."[14] Appiah is pointing out the crucial core of Wiredu's position that African philosophy need not claim uniqueness (in terms of its methods or problems considered) to be acceptable to the world. During his long academic career spanning three continents, Kwasi Wiredu has articulated this view in his conference speeches, articles, and books. Wiredu is best known for his 1980 book *Philosophy and an African Culture.*[15] The common theme in that collection of essays is that the fruitful way to engage in African philosophy is to critically reconstruct Africa's oral traditions to uncover the philosophical thinking therein. Utilizing the literary and scientific resources of the modern world does not make the effort any less African. Further, Wiredu holds that traditional thought is not peculiarly African. In the essay "How Not to Compare African Traditional Thought with Western Thought," Wiredu argues:

> It is of importance to try to understand how each mode of thought, and especially the traditional, functions in the total context of its society. Since African societies are among the closest approximations in the modern world to societies in the pre-scientific stage of development, the interest which anthropologists have shown in African thought is largely understandable. However, instead of seeing the basic non-scientific characteristics of African traditional thought as typifying traditional thought in general, Western anthropologists and others besides have mistakenly tended to take them as defining a peculiarly African way of thinking, with unfortunate effects.[16]

One of these "unfortunate effects" Wiredu laments is anachronism, which is the habit of holding on to values that have become outmoded. The nonscientific attitude attaches itself to values and habits not because these values and habits are effective in solving problems in a changing world, but rather because this is the way things have always been. In the technical, political, cultural, and ideological spheres, the cult of tradition opposes itself to modernity and change, continually striving to remold the present in the image of the past. Such an outlook militates against changes in worldview and hampers sociocultural and intellectual innovation. For these reasons Wiredu criticizes the negritude philosophers, anthropologists, and poets who define Africanity chiefly in terms of an unscientific, unanalytical, and untechnical African consciousness. Senghor in particular, as has been noted, espouses a negritude according to which the Negro African inherits from his or her ancestors a consciousness of the world in which the subject and object of observation, the natural and supernatural, and the material and spiritual are united inseparably. What Senghor articulates, and Wiredu rejects, is a theory that rests on an intrinsic and qualitative difference between the European and the Negro. It is precisely this difference that, according to Senghor, gives the European reason and logic, and the Negro soul and emotion. In denying Senghor's claim, Wiredu makes the clearest articulation of his view of philosophy:

> It should be noted, conversely, that the principle of rational evidence is not entirely absent from the thinking of the traditional African. Indeed, no society could survive for any length of time without basing a large part of its daily activities on beliefs derived from the evidence. You cannot farm without some rationally based knowledge of the soils, seeds, and climate; and no society can achieve any reasonable degree of harmony in human relations without the basic ability to assess claims and allegations by the method of objective investigating. The truth, then, is that rational knowledge is not the preserve of the modern West, nor is superstition a peculiarity of the African.[17]

For Wiredu, then, African thought must take its rightful place alongside the thought of other peoples of the world and reclaim the freedom to partake in logic and other rational procedures. Philosophy as an enterprise would not therefore change in its essence or methodologies in the context of Africa. Philosophy is universal.

Although universal, philosophy is never entirely divorced from culture, however. The kinds of questions the contemporary African is interested in arise out of the concrete situation of the continent. These questions themselves evolve with the culture. Traditional culture should be recorded and then critically interpreted. Philosophical thinking is exemplified not in the mere recording of traditions and cultures, but in the reconstruction of contemporary African culture as it has been influenced by Christian and Islamic customs and ideas. Wiredu is thus in agreement with Kenyan political scientist Ali A. Mazrui, who emphasizes, "Three civilizations have helped to shape contemporary Africa: Africa's rich indigenous inheritance, Islamic culture, and the impact of Western traditions and lifestyles."[18] This triple heritage makes it foolhardy for any philosopher or anthropologist to cling to the fiction of a "pure" or "real" traditional culture. The serious philosopher will seek to interpret traditional modes of life in the light of their interaction with science, technology, and industrialization. On the religious front, the syncretism of traditional religions and "modern" missionary religions is inescapable. The merging of Christianity, for example, with traditional African beliefs and practices played a role in the breakdown of those traditional societies and the emergence of new entities. In the same way we can today demonstrate persistent links between traditional African religions and contemporary nationalist movements that have been of immense political and military significance. One may look for examples of this syncretism in church designs and the incorporation of traditional instruments and songs into otherwise Western modes of worship, as well as African rituals and beliefs in the political arena. And on the philosophical front, some contemporary African philosophers challenge the traditional modes of being using their "alien" Western education and in this way give birth to new ways of thinking that are neither traditional nor Western. Wiredu's countryman and Ghana's first president, Kwame Nkrumah, gave an early indication of this trend in his philosophy of Consciencism, which he crafted from his study of Western philosophy at Lincoln University and the African values of community and mass participation. Julius Nyerere's idea of Ujamaa (Ujamaa is the Kiswahili word for "familyhood" and Nyerere's theory expresses his belief in the feeling of oneness or familyhood that Africans share) also exhibits the usual features of European socialism, although it too differs by emphasizing uniquely African features of communitarianism and hard work. In the cases of both Nyerere and Nkrumah, the end product is a version of socialism that is at the same time unique to Africa even as it bears a family resemblance to European socialisms.

Wiredu's work exhibits this same serious commitment to syncretism and borrowing in his use and interpretation of his native Akan tradition.

Wiredu himself has given ample evidence of how the contemporary African should approach the practice of philosophy.[19] In an article "On Defining African Philosophy," he repeats his main thesis:

> African philosophers are active today, trying (in some cases, at any rate) to achieve a synthesis of the philosophical insights of their ancestors with whatever they can extract of philosophical worth from the intellectual resources of the modern world. In truth, this is only one of their tasks; they are also reflecting on their languages and cultures in an effort to exploit their philosophical intimations. Besides all these, they are trying to grapple with some questions in such areas as logic, epistemology, and philosophy of science, which were not raised in their traditional culture. . . . It is in this way, and I think only in this way, that a tradition of modern philosophy can blossom in Africa.[20]

In his latest book, *Cultural Universals and Particulars: An African Perspective*, Wiredu gives evidence of how he has been promoting philosophy in Africa. Working primarily from his membership in the Akan ethnic group of West Africa, he uses elements of Akan thought as a springboard to a discussion of universal themes such as human communication, religion, custom and morality, language, truth, and human rights. Although his primary concerns remain the particular issues arising out of being an Akan and an African, his approach has its foundations in the universality of the methods of philosophy.

Paulin Hountondji on Philosophy as Writing

Paulin Hountondji (1942–), a philosopher from Bénin, has come to be regarded as one of the fiercest critics of ethnophilosophy and its implications about African separateness and difference. Hountondji targets modes of thinking that fail to deconstruct traditional African belief systems. Such thinking, in his view, perpetuates a colonial and neocolonial mentality that persistently sees Africa as a vast continent of "primitives" and "clan societies." Like Wiredu, Hountondji argues that the object and methods of philosophy are universal. As Wiredu also argues, what makes African philosophy African is not that it is about some unique African truths, concepts, or problems, but rather that it is the written literature of Africans engaged with universal philosophical problems. Just as one cannot talk meaningfully of a uniquely African science or technology, one cannot talk meaningfully of an African philosophy in the way attempted by ethnophilosophers. In their emphasis on African separateness, ethnophilosophers are basically trading in the currency of European stereotypes. Theirs is therefore, albeit unwittingly, a discourse carried on chiefly in Western and not African categories. The difference ethnophilosophers emphasize is difference from Europe. Similarly, the uniqueness and separateness so touted by ethnophilosophers is to be understood only as a reaction to Europe. It is clear to Hountondji that African ethnophilosophers, by failing to grasp the universality of philosophy, are acquiescing in their own subjugation by imperial forces, if unwittingly. I agree with Hountondji's assessment of ethnophilosophy as Eurocentric. Even though Hountondji is accurate in his assessment of ethnophilosophy, he can be criticized on other grounds. Curiously, his own procedure is equally as Eurocentric, although for different reasons. I will return to this criticism of his procedure in Chapter 4.

Hountondji thus rejects the view that there are specifically African truths or philosophical issues, and he further rejects the view that the commonly held beliefs of traditional African people can be regarded as philosophy:

> The problem, therefore, as regards our attitude towards our collective heritage, is how to respond to the challenge of cultural imperialism without imprisoning ourselves in an imaginary dialogue with Europe, how to re-evaluate our cultures without enslaving ourselves to them, how to restore the dignity of our past without giving room to a passeistic attitude. Instead of blindly condemning our traditions on behalf of reason, or rejecting the latter on behalf of the former, or making an absolute of the internal rationality of these traditions, it seems more reasonable to me to try and know our traditions as they were, beyond any mythology and distortion, not merely for the purpose of self-identification or justification, but in order to help us meet the challenges and problems of today.[21]

It would be a mistake to interpret Hountondji's view as a summary dismissal of the value of traditional African beliefs. An understanding of Africa and the traditional worldviews is important. There is value in recovering past traditions, but this value should not be overestimated, and the recovery of tradition is only the first step. Ethnophilosophers fail in the philosophical quest when they cast their gaze on the traditions of the "good old days" and ignore the historical and practical contexts of such backward looking. Ethnophilosophy is for Hountondji an "African pseudophilosophy," totally unreflexive and incapable of leading to a more meaningful African philosophy:

> Ethnophilosophy can now be seen in its true light. Because it has to account for an imaginary unanimity, to interpret a text which nowhere exists and has to be constantly reinvented, it is a science without an object, a 'crazed language' accountable to nothing, a discourse that has no referent, so that its falsity can never be demonstrated.[22]

Ethnophilosophy perpetuates the falsehood of an "African mind" or a "black consciousness" that posits that all members of a culture share a single awareness or experience because they share legends, myths, and proverbs. This confusion of traditions and worldviews with philosophy prompts Hountondji to add, "Ethnophilosophy is a pre-philosophy mistaking itself for a metaphilosophy, a philosophy which, instead of presenting its own rational justification, shelters lazily behind the authority of a tradition and projects its own theses and beliefs on that tradition."[23] These critiques of ethnophilosophy help clarify Hountondji's view of what constitutes African philosophy. Given the criticisms he has made, it becomes apparent that philosophy must for him consist in a critical examination that challenges the assumptions and categorizations that have been employed in the marginalization of Africa. By "African philosophy" Hountondji means:

> If we now return to our question, namely, whether philosophy resides in the worldview described or in the description itself, we can now assert that if it resides in either, it must be the second, the description of that vision, even if this is, in fact, a self-deluding invention that hides behind its own products. African philosophy does exist therefore, but in a new sense, as a literature produced by Africans and dealing with philosophical issues.[24]

Hountondji's has proved to be a most controversial definition of African philosophy. By stipulating that philosophy consists of the written literature by Africans, he rules out the oral tradition as a source of texts that can themselves remain open to sustained critical reflection. So for Hountondji literacy is presupposed by philosophy. Such a definition of philosophy implies that writing is the crucial determinant of whether a philosophy exists. Embedded in this insistence on writing is the further controversy about whether the oral literatures of Africa are legitimate philosophical texts comparable to the written texts of Europe. His position raises questions that we shall defer until Chapter 4.

For Hountondji, African philosophy is addressed to Africans. Even as ethnophilosophy served the purposes of Europe in its colonization of Africa, so should an African philosophy which is both critical and reconstructive serve the purposes of a contemporary Africa. The geographical origin of the writers and the audience for whom these writers write become essential points in defining African philosophy. Under this definition, the works of the ethnophilosophers and the negritude poets and philosophers must be excluded from consideration as African philosophy because their audience was the European public. By the same token, literature by Africans that is not even directly engaged in "African philosophy" counts as African philosophy despite that content.

Hountondji views philosophy as critical discourse that needs the firm foundation of science because only the culture of science makes it possible to question old ideas and discard them in the light of new ones. For a development of this theme of science as the basis of African philosophy, I refer the reader to Hountondji's *African Philosophy: Myth and Reality*.[25] In developing his critique of ethnophilosophy, Hountondji seems taken by the claims of science to objectivity. Scientific objectivity is for him advantageous in two ways. This first advantage is that science makes it possible for an impartial observer to make judgments untainted by cultural perspective or experience. The second advantage is the assumption that science makes of one true reality which is accessible to anyone in the right frame of mind. Hountondji does not seem to sufficiently appreciate a point made in much contemporary feminist writing about how oppressive this unselfconscious adoption of a supposedly objective scientific perspective may be. I revisit this criticism of Hountondji in Chapter 3. For him, a method similar to that of science is the only way forward for African philosophy. And Hountondji argues that contemporary Africans have just begun the written exchanges between themselves that over time will result in establishing the critical discourse worthy of the name African philosophy.

Henry Odera Oruka on Philosophical Sagacity

A universalist conception of philosophy of a different kind has been offered by the late Kenyan philosopher Henry Odera Oruka (1939–1995). Odera Oruka joins Wiredu and Hountondji in highlighting the critical aspects of the enterprise of philosophy. He distinguishes between philosophy in a strict sense and philosophy in a debased sense. In the strict sense, philosophy unearths hidden assumptions, implications, and contradictions in human experience. Philosophy in the debased sense limits itself to the contours of traditional worldviews or cultures. Since ethnophilosophy does not meet the strict standard, it is therefore philosophy only in the debased sense. Communal outlooks about magic, cosmology, or ethics do not properly constitute philosophical thinking.

Whereas Hountondji argues that oral tradition is incapable of sustaining critical thought and exchange, Odera Oruka argues against the idea that philosophy presupposes literacy. The basis of his view is research conducted over a period of twenty years into a trend in African philosophy he called Sage philosophy, or simply Sagacity. The result of that long research is *Sage Philosophy: Indigenous Thinkers and Modern Debate on African Philosophy*.[26] His thesis was that within Africa's oral traditions there are nonliterate sages of two kinds: those who are unable to rise above the level of culture philosophy and those who exhibit all the philosophical abilities of a Socrates. Culture philosophy is for Odera Oruka philosophy in the debased sense, and the sages who engage in it can at best be only folk sages or culture sages. A folk sage has mastery of the communal outlook, above which he or she never rises. For the folk or culture sage,

> Beliefs or truth-claims within a culture philosophy are generally treated as "absolutes." Anything outside or contradictory to the culture is treated with indifference and even hostility. Those sages or persons who are experts in the culture defend this philosophy and the structure of their society with the zeal of fanatical ideologists defending the political line.[27]

What this means is that culture sages, like the ethnophilosophers, are guilty of mistaking culture for philosophy. Such a mere cataloging of the traditions of any culture can at best provide only the worldviews of that culture. It is not philosophy in the strict sense, but a culture philosophy

that does not rise above communal worldviews and religious conceptions.

In contrast to culture sages, there are philosophical sages. Of their
enterprise, Odera Oruka writes:

> Philosophic sagacity, however, is often a product and a re-
> flective reevaluation of the culture philosophy. The few sages
> who possess the philosophic inclination make a critical assess-
> ment of their culture and its underlying beliefs. Using the
> power of reason rather than the celebrated beliefs of the com-
> munal consensus and explanation, the sage philosopher pro-
> duces a system within a system, and order within an order.[28]

The result of Sagacity is critical effort, which is the property of individuals rather than the community at large. It is that feature that Odera
Oruka takes to distinguish what he calls Sagacity from ethnophilosophy.
To be knowledgeable about, and merely to express, one's cultural traits
is useful. But for Odera Oruka, as for Hountondji, ethnophilosophy is a
prelude to philosophy. To seek causal explanations, to engage in interpretation with a view to transformation when the occasion calls for it—
these are second-order activities. For Odera Oruka, then, philosophy is
the exercise of subjecting one's cultural world to the standard of reason.
Although philosophy is universal, African philosophy originates in African culture in the sense that historical and social realities of the continent
provide the experiences upon which the sages and other philosophers
theorize.

The crucial features of philosophy Odera Oruka emphasizes are critical interpretation of culture and the individuality of that interpretation.
Whereas philosophy may begin at the level of culture, it should not end
there. Culture must in turn be subject to scrutiny and, if necessary, a
transformative reconstruction. Odera Oruka's universalist perspective
challenges the ethnophilosophers and their claim that philosophy can be
geographically unique or culture specific. Philosophy must be a personal, second-order activity that is universal in its methodology.

Sagacity as an approach in African philosophy is just beginning to
receive increased critical attention. Professor Jay M. van Hook in "Kenyan Sage Philosophy: A Review and Critique"[29] noted ongoing M.A.
and Ph.D. dissertations on Sagacity. His own challenge, which I support,
is that African philosophers continue to make this trend a living tradition
of African philosophy by debating its definitions (of folk philosophy,

culture philosophy, sage philosophy, and philosophic sagacity), by scruti-
nizing the methods used to identify sages, and by examining the rational
justifications offered by the sages for their opinions. In 1997, a tribute to
Odera Oruka, *Sagacious Reasoning: Henry Odera Oruka in Memoriam*,[30]
was published. This collection of Odera Oruka's essays and commentar-
ies by a diverse group of scholars clearly indicates the many directions in
which future research on Sagacity may be taken.

Hermeneutical Orientations

Philosophers in the hermeneutical tradition have challenged both ethnophilosophical and universalist perspectives. These philosophers take
African traditions as their starting point. Rooting themselves in what is
traditional to Africa, they seek to escape an enslavement to the past by
using that past to open up the future. Philosophy properly construed
must move beyond a preoccupation with ethnological considerations
and universalist abstraction and call into question the real relations of
power in Africa. The works of Tsenay Serequeberhan, Marcien Towa,
and Okonda Okolo exemplify this hermeneutical orientation in African
philosophy.

Tsenay Serequeberhan: Philosophy in Service of Liberation

In his first book, *African Philosophy: The Essential Readings*,[31] the Eritrean
philosopher Tsenay Serequeberhan (1952–) sketched his view on the
debate about whether an African philosophy exists and how it is to be
defined. In that sketch he staked out the following position:

> The discourse of African philosophy is thus directly and his-
> torically linked to the demise of European hegemony (colo-
> nialism and neocolonialism) and is aimed at fulfilling/
> completing this demise. It is a reflective and critical effort to
> rethink the African situation beyond the confines of Euro-
> centric concepts and categories. In this indigenized context,
> furthermore, questions of "class struggle" (the "universal"
> concern of Marxist theory!) and the empowerment of the
> oppressed can fruitfully be posed and engaged.[32]

Serequeberhan here proposes a different conception of African philosophy from those of the universalists and the ethnophilosophers—
conceptions that had, in his opinion, failed to emphasize the African
liberation struggle as the proper concern of African philosophy. His in-

troductory article "African Philosophy: The Point in Question" stakes
out a position that defines African philosophy by focusing on the inter-
pretative character of philosophy. It is, however, in his second book, *The
Hermeneutics of African Philosophy: Horizon and Discourse*,[33] that Serequeberhan works out his view in greater detail. More than semantic issues
are at stake. African cultural, political, and economic life is at stake too.
His definition of African philosophy is set in the context of a continent
grappling with the problem of how to go about the business of liberating
itself from European cultural, economic, linguistic, political, and ideological violence. Insofar as the universalists uncritically appropriate European definitions of philosophy and the ethnophilosophers avoid the
political questions posed by the historicity of the African situation, both
approaches fail to apprehend that European violence against Africa
should be the central question in African philosophy. Ethnophilosophy
preoccupies itself mostly with cataloging and documenting the worldviews of Africa. The universalists find little that is unique to Africa that
is philosophical in the strict sense. Ethnophilosophy unduly exalts the
African past and confuses culture with philosophy. A universalist orientation valorizes rigor for rigor's sake and uncritically accepts European
frameworks.

For Serequeberhan, therefore, only a hermeneutical approach that
takes lived experience as its starting point is capable of making any substantive contribution to African philosophy. The hermeneutical approach becomes imperative in postcolonial Africa because the specific
needs of the time are the struggle for liberation from neocolonialism,
the struggle to become human by contesting subordination, repression,
and social exploitation. It is the struggle to reclaim the continent's history even as that history is being made. This understanding would be
what makes the difference between the hermeneutical approach and the
other approaches, for, as Serequeberhan notes:

> In view of all of the above, then, and beyond the initial mo-
> ment of counter-violence, the African liberation struggle is
> an originative process through which the historicity of the
> colonized is reclaimed and appropriated anew. . . . Thus, in
> contradistinction to Senghor and ethnophilosophy, on the
> one hand, and Nkrumah, Hountondji, and Professional Phi-
> losophy, on the other, this will be our hermeneutical response
> to the question: what are the people of Africa trying to free
> themselves from and what are they trying to establish?[34]

The hermeneutical approach of Serequeberhan conceives of effective history as an open-ended struggle, a struggle calling for constant vigilance and a critical assessment of its own shortcomings. There is a lot in Serequeberhan's view that is reminiscent of the views of the universalist philosophers. We find the same refrain that African philosophy is to be distinguished from the puerile hankering after a glorious past, the mere reappropriation of traditions or the recouping of values that is characteristic of the ethnophilosophers. Serequeberhan, however, adds the proviso that African philosophy is also to be distinguished from the uncritical appropriation of Western canons and Eurocentric horizons seen in so many of the early African philosophers. Indeed, "philosophy is inherently and in its very nature a hermeneutics of the existentiality of human existence."[35] Ethnophilosophy and professional philosophy thus exhibit, from a hermeneutical standpoint, a deeper and far more dangerous failing: they fail to come to terms with the inescapable violence that has characterized the intercourse of Europe with Africa. Without apprehending the cultural, economic, and ideological aspects of this violence, it is impossible to fully answer that all-important question, What are the people of Africa trying to free themselves from and what are they trying to establish? Serequeberhan very clearly answers this question. Africans are trying to free themselves from European categories and the propensity to unwittingly embrace a Eurocentric worldview. What they are trying to establish is their historicity and with it a philosophic practice that is both reflective and reflexive, a practice that focuses on lived experience. African philosophy, on this view, entails by its very nature a recourse to violence:

> In this respect it has to be emphasized that the colonized does not choose violence. Violence is not a choice. It is the condition of existence imposed on the colonized by the colonizer, which enforces the colonized's status of being a "native," a *thing*, a historical being forcefully barred from history. In other words, the direct confrontation between the colonizer and the colonized is not the beginning of violence in the colonial situation. The "continued agony of the colonized" is in fact the historically grounding violence of colonialism.[36]

There is no room in African philosophy, it seems, for advocating nonviolent outlooks. Those engaged in this enterprise need only ask themselves which violence they bring to the struggle. One brings either the all-pervading violence of the colonizer who insists on molding everything in his own image, a violence that spawns theories that implicitly or explicitly celebrate the demise of the non-European. Or one brings the liberating counterviolence of the formerly colonized, a counterviolence that establishes one's historicity by bringing into question the European texts and traditions so forcefully imposed on the colonized. Philosophy has the task of carefully deconstructing these texts and traditions, critically rejecting the mind-set steeped in European categories.

Marcien Towa: Philosophy with a Pragmatic Flavor

Like Hountondji, Marcien Towa (1931–)is another philosopher from West Africa—Hountondji from Bénin, Towa from Cameroon. Conceptually, however, Towa is closer to Serequeberhan. He doubts that the preoccupations of the ethnophilosophers are properly philosophical. With an audience that is not primarily African, ethnophilosophy is imprisoned in its own particularity and is not well placed to ask how Africa's future may best be harnessed utilizing the past. In his *Essai sur la Problematique Philosophique dans l'Afrique actuelle*,[37] Towa denounces the brand of Africanity espoused by Senghor and the negritude poets and "philosophers" as an Africanity that is an unwitting validation of European prejudices. The negritude movement thus became a mouthpiece through which European stereotypes of Africa were propagated. By reaching into the African past and stressing values like emotion and irrationalism (or at least the deemphasizing of logic and reason), Senghor and others play into the hands of the West while abandoning claim to the secret of European power—the intellect. African philosophy is powerless and meaningless if it cannot be a means of constructing the future. A genuine African philosophy is one that in its engagement in the struggle against domination exhibits a pragmatic flavor. Otherwise, it is nothing more than a tool of domination. Towa clarifies his view of philosophy thus:

> In this sense, African philosophy is the exercise by Africans of a specific type of intellectual activity (the critical examination of fundamental problems) applied to the African reality. The type of intellectual activity in question is, as such, neither African, European, Greek, nor German; it is philosophy in general. What is African are the men of flesh and bones who are and who evoke the problems of supreme importance and on whom these same problems are applicable immediately.[38]

Here Towa gives a definition of African philosophy that greatly resembles the universalist approach of Hountondji. Towa, however, rejects Hountondji's predication of philosophy on writing because if one follows Hountondji, one would have to deny out of hand the existence of precolonial African philosophy. Towa finds Hountondji's position unwittingly converging with that of Africa's erstwhile colonizers who considered Africans primitive and completely innocent of philosophy. According to Towa, Hountondji's strategy fails because it now reduces Africans themselves to defending Western stereotypes about the lack of philosophical complexity in traditional Africa. Such an exclusion also cuts itself off from tapping any genuine contribution to African originality before the advent of literacy. Hountondji's choice is a costly one because traditional cultures too have contributions to make to philosophy, as Towa notes:

> Philosophy expresses itself essentially in discourse, oral or written, and it is from this discourse that one has to start, that is to say, from texts. The first task of the historians of African thought consequently consists in establishing a corpus of texts congruent with the adopted definition of philosophy and making this available to researchers.[39]

The admission of the oral as text is crucial because that inclusion beefs up the hermeneutical arsenal in its combat with Western ethnocentrism. It is a part of the arsenal that must, however, be used with extreme caution. Towa warns:

> We are not in agreement with Hountondji, who wants to exclude oral texts. After all, Socrates did not write anything. That is not enough reason to pretend that he is not a philosopher. The ethnophilosophers, on the contrary, utilize any cultural element indiscriminately. They interrogate rituals, myths (without discrimination), art, poetry, language, social, political, and educational institutions, etc., on the pretext that philosophy is incarnated in the life of a people.[40]

The extremes represented by Hountondji and the ethnophilosophers are to be avoided. The only kinds of meaningful oral texts are those that will make a contribution to the political and economic rejuvenation of Africa. Ethnophilosophers make the mistake of going overboard in their acceptance of anything cultural as philosophically meaningful. What Towa suggests is a careful sifting through the oral literary texts for inconsistencies, irrelevancies, and untruths. Only the texts that survive this test can be relied upon to contribute to making Africa powerful again. Thus the aim of going to the past is not nostalgia. The ultimate project is to assimilate and integrate aspects of the cultural past into a program for progress.

Now, in Europe, the secret of progress and control of the environment has been the abandonment of traditional values that impede philosophical synthesis and free thinking, while at the same time cultivating those values that aid science and technology. If Africans are to gain control of their environment, philosophers must help in the process of developing worldviews that integrate philosophy and science. The task of African philosophy is thus to start from traditional African cultures and build bridges between the past and the present in ways that are not limiting.

Okonda Okolo: Interpreting Traditions as Texts

In his "Tradition and Destiny: Horizons of an African Philosophical Hermeneutics,"[41] Okonda Okolo (1947–) advances a line of reasoning much as we have seen in Towa, whom he does not mention directly. He explicitly associates his work with that of Nigerian Theophilus Okere[42] and Zairean Nkombe Oleko.[43] They all have in common the interpretation of culture and tradition as their point of departure. As with Towa, the proper task of philosophy is to interpret texts with a view to taking back control of one's destiny. Again in agreement with Towa, Okolo writes:

> The African tradition is the text of our reading. But first, what is a text? One should not limit the text to a written text. We have to retain the lesson of contemporary hermeneutic theories and extend the sense of a text to include all verbal concatenations ([enchainment]) and all that offers itself to be read, that is to say, tradition as a whole.[44]

This is not, however, a call for the indiscriminate embrace of tradition that characterizes the ethnophilosophers, in Okolo's opinion. The embrace of the oral as text must be understood in the context of a people's historicity. That text is replete with internal tensions and contradictions. It is in the careful analysis and sifting through of those tensions and contradictions that one comes to a self-awareness. The ways in which those who share a culture see their universe are embedded within their language(s). The oral texts will thus reveal conflicting visions—some of these visions lending themselves more easily than others to manipulation of the future. Interpretation must have the component of always being forward-looking even as it is grounded in the past. That past, as every African should know, contains a history of harm done by Europe to the African. If there are aspects of the oral tradition that continue to help this colonization, those should be abandoned. Only those aspects that alleviate the suffering qualify as texts. Traditions that allow old problems to remain unsolved impede the emancipatory process. Okolo highlights this problem of lacking control of one's destiny:

> It is, for example, Christianity that generally determines the problematic of a religious and theological "retake"; it is Occidental philosophy that often constitutes the basis of the philosophical "retake" of the African tradition. Whereas it is the African tradition itself that ought to assure the hermeneuticity, the philosophicity, and hence the Africanity of a determined practice.[45]

Therein lies the charter to an emancipatory African philosophy. The dominant ideological, social, and religious narratives about Africa have been from outside Africa. These are narratives in which indigenous African experience enjoys a very low rating. Such has been the legacy of Europe. The practice of Christianity in Africa, for example, reveals assumptions about the superiority of the doctrines of that religion in comparison to the traditional African religions. Indeed, during the struggles for political independence on the continent, Christian teachings about giving to Caesar his due tended to have an inhibiting effect on efforts toward liberation. In the areas of economic organization and systems of government, there was the same pernicious influence of alien notions. The hermeneutic approach brings to the fore the many habits of thought that have been internalized for so long as well as the vested interests of those who have gained much by foisting these habits of thought on Africa. If one accepts the truism that Africa has suffered immense exploitation at the hands of Europe, Okolo's definition of African philosophy revolves around a practice that brings to an end the exploitation of Africa by Europe, and indeed a practice that employs African traditions in the service of that liberation.

Various Classifications of African Philosophy

A Tripartite Scheme
With such divergent definitions of philosophy it is no wonder there is little agreement about the meaning and existence of African philosophy. At the beginning of this chapter I characterized philosophy as a process (rather than a fixed body of knowledge) that yields a tentative body of knowledge that embodies principles and judgments based on a knowledge of the social and material reality available at the time—a body of knowledge that is itself under constant review, interpretation, and analysis. Following that definition, my own reading of the writings in African philosophy would be to divide them into three categories: ethnophilosophical approaches, universalist definitions, and hermeneutical orientations. Let me here give a sense of where other African philosophers would fall within this tripartite scheme.

Ethnophilosophical Approaches
Among the ethnophilosophers, we have already mentioned Tempels, Kagame, and Senghor. In Chapter 2 we look also at John Mbiti and Marcel Griaule. These are not controversial inclusions because the anthologies in African philosophy already categorize these authors as ethnophilosophers. The controversial addition I would like to make to the class of ethnophilosophical writers is the Senegalese scholar Cheikh Anta Diop. His immense scholarship is a response to the European denial of an African literate past. Further, he condemns as false and even dangerous the idea that oral traditions should not be respected. For Diop, Africans tell, sing, dance, sculpt, and paint their history. He reconstructs African history to make known to the world African ways of governing and being governed; unique social, economic, and religious roles; and African approaches to architecture, metallurgy, glassmaking, medicine, weaving, agriculture, and hunting.[46] Two former presidents, Julius Nyerere of Tanzania and Kwame Nkrumah of Ghana, like Diop, would be similarly controversial additions to the ethnophilosophical scheme because they are usually classified otherwise by other African philosophers and also because their inclusion threatens, in the opinion of some, to make the ethnophilosophical category too broad. Odera Oruka, for example, classifies both Nyerere and Nkrumah under the trend he calls "Nationalist-Ideological" because their works arise out of their political commitments. Nonetheless, the risk my classification takes seems acceptable to me because the writings of Nyerere and Nkrumah show an

affinity with the main features of ethnophilosophy. In Nyerere's concept of *Ujamaa* one detects an idea that would generalize family to include the different levels of clan, nation, and finally continent. It is a concept that has its roots in a timeless collective unconscious worldview. Nkrumah's "African personality" is formed only through relationships with others and entails the collective character of the group. In those respects Nkrumah and Nyerere are strikingly similar. Both again predicate their positions on a shared reality and African values. In spite of material differences between Nyerere's Tanzania and Nkrumah's Ghana, both writers adhere to some form of "African socialism" that is the articulation of a communitarian ideal. It is not an ideal that the ordinary African reaches by conscious purposive thought. In their articulations, Nyerere and Nkrumah do not claim to be producing *their* own philosophies. They are reporting and building on shared African values—which is indeed what ethnophilosophy is. In this passage, Nkrumah removes doubt that he fits the ethnophilosophical scheme:

> Consciencism is the map in intellectual terms of the disposition of forces which will enable African society to digest the Western and the Islamic and the Euro-Christian elements in Africa, and develop them in such a way that they fit the African personality. The African personality is itself defined by the cluster of humanist principles which underlie the traditional African society. Philosophical Consciencism is that philosophical standpoint which taking its start from the present content of the African conscience, indicates the way in which progress is forged out of the conflict in that conscience.[47]

Universalist Definitions

In addition to Wiredu, Hountondji, and Odera Oruka, for whom reason is universal, I would include Peter Bodunrin in this category of universalist African philosophers.[48] Bodunrin doubts that a philosophical tradition can arise in the absence of literacy, more so since it is literacy that makes possible sustained rigor and systematization. If philosophy is not universal, it is not philosophy. So too one would have to include Kwame Gyekye,[49] who finds that metaphysics is the core of Western philosophy just as it is in African thought. To deny African peoples the ability to engage in philosophical thought is to imply that they are unable to reflect on or conceptualize their experience about God, being, the nature of personhood, destiny, free will, and causality. It is indeed to deny that Africans are as human as everyone else. Father Innocent Onyewuenyi[50] too points to a concerted effort on the part of Western scholars to deny Africa any contribution in the field of philosophy. In common with the other universalists, he holds that even though every culture has its own worldviews, philosophizing is a universal experience. Any denial of abstract thought to African peoples, and any predication of philosophy on writing (even in the ways favored by some universalists like Hountondji) are nothing more than attempts to establish European experiences as the standard for all philosophizing.

Hermeneutical Orientations

In addition to Serequeberhan, Towa, and Okolo, we may add to this category some non-African writers. Frantz Fanon, though born in Martinique, wrote *Les Damnés de la Terre* (appearing in English as *The Wretched of the Earth*)[51] out of his experience practicing psychiatry at a French government hospital in Algeria. Although Fanon makes no explicit references to African philosophy, he addresses the issues of colonization, the anticolonial liberation struggle, and the consequences of postcolonization and neocolonialism in the context of contemporary Africa. A central theme of the book and also of his other books is the tension between two groups—a group committed to the needs and aspirations of the vast majority of the people of a given nation, and a group that comprises the privileged class. It is a tension and conflict between the colonizer (not necessarily of foreign origin) and the marginalized. Fanon writes about the violence by which a people are denied the possibility of self-determination on the political, economic, and cultural levels and reduced to the level of objects. Beyond posing the problem, Fanon's work exhibits a strong hermeneutical element that calls into question the processes and criteria by which groups gain hegemony over others, and thus perpetuate inequality. The aim of analysis is helping in the struggle for independence, the fight for emancipation. In the liberation movement, traditional African culture may be of assistance—not, however, in the blind sense of losing oneself in the traditional ritual and symbolism of one's people. Fanon, like the other philosophers whose orientation is hermeneutical, is severely critical of the retreat from reason exemplified by negritude. Negritude, in his opinion, resembles a stage of colonialism in which the colonized tries to prove, by identifying with the past, the value of and difference between the colonizer and the colonized. The disadvantages of this strategy are that it utilizes a methodology similar to that of the colonizer—only this time the methodology is politically impotent because it does not bring about any change in the power relations. Cultural pride merely for the sake of difference is an instrument in neither cultural nor political battles of liberation. Fanon's work, in contrast, has become virtually a road map for freedom fighters around the world, an instrument to help peoples of the world in forging their own sense of identity.

In a similar hermeneutical vein, the work of African American philosopher Lucius Outlaw fits the scheme. In many of his published articles, but especially in "African Philosophy: Deconstructive and Reconstructive Challenges,"[52] he sets out to challenge illicit assumptions that block the liberation of black people. From a comparativist standpoint, Outlaw reveals concerns very similar to those of contemporary African philosophers. His aim in this article is limited to answering the question, Is there an African philosophy? First, however, he calls into question the question itself. His deconstructive project reveals that the question is really one of whether Africans are as human as the rest of humanity. The question cannot be answered satisfactorily if one theorizes within what he calls the "Euro-American philosophical agenda." Outlaw proposes that people of African descent must in the first instance be involved in the effort to displace Eurocentric notions of "man" and "civilized human." In a move that reveals his socialist foundations, he laments the difficulty of doing this within a capitalist social order. Thus the critical orientation to reclaim cultural, economic, and political humanity ought to be tempered with a humanistic socialism. Indeed, in "African, African American, Africana Philosophy,"[53] Outlaw advocates a way forward for Africana philosophy to forge a unity in its agenda and praxis, and to succeed in combat against "pernicious racism and ethnocentrism."

African liberation needs to be undertaken on a number of different fronts. The work of V. Y. Mudimbe, especially his seminal *The Invention of Africa*,[54] draws attention to how the "pernicious racism and ethnocentrism" described by Outlaw have long been in practice in the realms of the language and the concepts with which Europe attempts to understand Africa. The Africa one encounters in European scholarship is an invention—a mirror image of Europe, an image whose peculiarity is that it reflects the inversion of European values. Africa as European invention is characterized by all that is evil and negative about Europe. Mudimbe's charge to contemporary African intellectuals is therefore clear. The hermeneutical task must involve bringing into question these pernicious inventions.

The Four Trends by Henry Odera Oruka

The tripartite scheme I favor, and that I have outlined here, is not the dominant one among African philosophers. The most widely cited classificatory schema is that of Henry Odera Oruka, which identifies four trends in African philosophy:[55] ethnophilosophy, philosophic Sagacity, nationalist-ideological philosophy, and "critical" or Professional philosophy.

Ethnophilosophy, as we have noted, sees African philosophy as communal thought, relying heavily on myths, legends, traditions, and other cultural forms. Odera Oruka's preferred view of philosophy is that it is a critical enterprise and because ethnophilosophy does not meet this strict standard it should not be regarded as philosophy. Ethnophilosophy can at best only be philosophy in a debased sense because communal outlooks about magic, cosmology, or ethics do not constitute philosophy in the proper sense. Examples of ethnophilosophical approaches Odera Oruka mentions are Marcel Griaule's *Conversations with Ogotemmeli* and the type of research conducted among traditional Yoruba medicine men (*onisegun*) by J. O. Sodipo and Barry Hallen. Other representative ethnophilosophers are Tempels, Kagame, Mbiti, and Senghor.

Philosophic Sagacity is not to be confused with ethnophilosophy since it is a reflective enterprise that reevaluates culture philosophy. Moreover, that reevaluation is achieved without benefit of writing or contact with Europe. It is African philosophy in the strict sense. Examples of philosophic sages that Odera Oruka gives from his extended research in Kenya are Paul Mbuya K'Akoko and Oruka Ranginya. They and another sage, Chege Kamau, are among those who were interviewed to test the Sagacity hypothesis; these interviews are published in Odera Oruka's *Sage Philosophy: Indigenous Thinkers and Modern Debate on African Philosophy.*[56] Chege Kamau is given as an example of a folk sage. To recapitulate an earlier discussion, the difference between philosophic and folk sages is explainable thus: the former engage in rational critiques of their culture, pointing out its inconsistencies, while the latter are merely skilled at articulating communal belief.

Nationalist-ideological philosophy is represented by the political writings that incorporate the communitarian values of traditional African life. These also fall short of being philosophy in the true sense for Odera Oruka, although he does not deny that the mostly political and cultural works arising out of the struggle against colonialism are potentially rich sources of African philosophy. A lot of critical work, however, still needs to be done before any philosophy is crafted out of the traditional values of family and communalism. Hence writers such as Amilcar Cabral, Sekou Toure, Julius Nyerere, and Kwame Nkrumah (who according to Odera Oruka's classificatory scheme all belong to the nationalist-ideological trend) have made a significant initial contribution by providing texts for that philosophical task.

Lastly, Professional philosophy designates that class of African philosophers, trained in Western philosophy, who share a rejection of ethnophilosophy and adopt universalist definitions of philosophy. Their practice therefore tends to exude a Euro-American feel. These philosophers tend to differ widely in their stances regarding the subject matter of philosophy or its methodologies. They are united, however, in the belief that philosophy must have the same meaning in all cultures, even though the epistemological, metaphysical, and ethical questions prioritized in these cultures will be different. Odera Oruka classifies together such diverse thinkers as Paulin Hountondji, Peter Bodunrin, and Kwasi Wiredu. Following the criteria he has laid down, we would have to include the contemporary African philosophers Tsenay Serequeberhan, Marcien Towa, and Lansana Keita as Professional philosophers.[57] It would seem that the one thing Professional philosophers have in common is that their livelihood comes from the practice of philosophy. Even though they belong to different schools of thought, they nonetheless are forging a tradition within African philosophy of sustained exchanges in avenues such as symposia, academic journals, and books.

The Three Phases by Lansana Keita

Lansana Keita is among those philosophers Odera Oruka classified as Professional. He disagrees with Odera Oruka on how to define African philosophy and especially on whether philosophic Sagacity should count as philosophy at all. Keita takes an essentially hermeneutical approach in his view of the task of African philosopher. He writes, "the theoreticians of philosophy in an African context must attempt to construct a modern African philosophy with the notion that its formulation would be geared towards helping in the development of a modern African civilization."[58]

It is not enough, it seems, to adopt a definition of philosophy that stresses the speculative and personal dimensions of the discipline. For philosophy to serve as an agent of change, the individual reflections of the philosophers must be set within a context in which they aid in the self-awareness of individuals and societies who in turn are confronted with existence under conditions that are not static. Philosophers should evaluate their parameters of judgment, conceptual frameworks, and existential attitudes and values in the light of changing historical conditions. Philosophy is thus culture-dependent to the extent that it is a self-consciousness of culture. The following effort is necessary if one wishes to get to the truly philosophical within a culture:

> It would be an error, therefore, for the philosopher in the African context to assume that philosophy as it is practiced in the Western world should serve as a model for the practice of philosophy. A useful approach, it seems, would be to regard philosophical activity as engaging in theoretical analysis of issues and ideas of practical concern. But in modern society it is the social and natural sciences that discuss ideas and issues relevant to practical concerns. Thus the practice of philosophy in the African context should be concerned first with the analysis of the methodology and content of the social sciences, i.e. history, economics, anthropology, political science, etc., for it is the methodology of research of a given discipline that determines the orientation of research in that discipline and the kinds of solutions to problems ultimately proposed.[59]

This is the route by which Keita comes to his position on African philosophy. In the manner of Hountondji and Towa, Keita realizes and emphasizes the role of science in transforming the social and material world. At the same time, he does not want to deny ancient Africa a philosophical tradition. Like Hountondji, Keita predicates philosophy on writing. Yet like the hermeneutical philosophers, he wants to incorporate into philosophy that which was useful in traditional African thought systems. In "The African Philosophical Tradition,"[60] he navigates a position that finds an old philosophical tradition in Africa but limits that tradition to written texts. Descriptive comments about traditional belief systems, such as the ethnophilosophers deal in, are not genuinely philosophical. Keita does not mean to ignore these belief systems nor to discount the possibility of mining or teasing out of these oral traditions some universal philosophical problems. His point is that a descriptive exercise per se contributes little to confronting the social world and even less to societal transformation. Traditional belief systems, and descriptions of them, prove vital only when they are employed in the direction of contemporary development and in the promotion of a technological orientation.

For Keita, development and technology are supportable only through a medium such as writing. It is therefore in the written text that we must look for African philosophy. If we define philosophy as critical, written thought, the philosophical tradition in Africa extends as far back as the ancient Egyptians and the scholarly works in medieval Africa. Keita divides that tradition into three phases: *ancient or classical African philosophy*, *medieval African philosophy*, and *modern African philosophy*.

The *Hermetica*, a collection of treatises written in Greek, and supposed to contain Egyptian philosophy translated into Greek, is representative of the ancient or classical phase. Akhenaten's cosmological revolution circa 1300 B.C. is among Keita's evidence of African philosophy during this period.

The medieval phase centers around the old kingdoms of Ghana, Mali, and Songhai and the impressive intellectual achievement of Islamic scholarship in those kingdoms. That scholarship exhibits an attempt to identify, confront, and refine the intellectual and cultural legacy of the time. Keita gives no examples of representative texts.

During the modern period, contemporary Africa is attempting to establish a firm technological base. The African problematic thus requires of contemporary philosophy an orientation that grapples with issues facing the contemporary African state. Keita disparages this phase for its paucity of written critical thought. He finds "no systematic body of knowledge expanded by African philosophers today that could be rightly labelled African philosophy."[61] African philosophers are not completely to blame for this because the absence of philosophy is one of the lingering effects of colonialism.

Keita's classification is obviously controversial, for he directly enters into the debate about whether Greek philosophy originated from ancient Egypt. From the claim that Egyptian philosophy predates Greek (and therefore European) philosophy, further controversial implications arise. One possibility is that Greek philosophy was stolen from Egypt (given their subsequent similarity). In that case we must further inquire into the motives of those ancient Greeks who appropriated ancient Egyptian wisdom without any acknowledgment whatsoever. Another possibility is that Egypt was the mother of Western civilization— Egyptian thought having given birth to philosophy, cultivated democracy, and encouraged scientific outlooks. In this latter case we must revise our ideas of what counts as "European civilization." Keita's scheme highlights the complex dimensions of the classificatory process. The quest to define African philosophy has, in addition to the academic/scholarly function, profound political and psychological implications.

That is why it is easy, if care is not taken, for a classificatory scheme to be seen as taking sides in the Afrocentric versus Eurocentric debate. Inevitably, we must ask of any classification, Is it a truer account than other classifications? Of the many classifications to choose from, we must ask which we are to prefer. Innocent though these questions first appear, they lead deep into political waters.

The different classificatory schemas reveal the commitments of their proponents—commitments to ideas about what constitutes philosophy, to notions of text, to political and ideological stands. Contrast Odera Oruka's commitments with Marcien Towa's. Both are in agreement that the preoccupations of the ethnophilosophers are not properly philosophical. Both charge ethnophilosophers with inadvertently mistaking culture for philosophy. For both Odera Oruka and Towa, a mere cataloging of the traditions of any culture can at best provide only the worldviews of that culture—thus amounting to philosophy only in the debased or diluted sense of culture philosophy. Towa's hermeneutical inclinations reject such an enslavement to the past while Odera Oruka's universalist approach does not allow for the equation of worldviews or religious conceptions with philosophy. Even as they agree on what African philosophy is not, they are led in different directions in their search for its genuine content. Towa considers African philosophy genuine when it appropriates the past in the effort to deal with current problems on the continent with a view to influencing or shaping the future. Since such a philosophy must be practical, it is not surprising, then, that Towa sees African philosophy as beginning with the publication of Kwame Nkrumah's *Consciencism* in 1970. Nkrumah's subtitle "Philosophy and Ideology for Decolonization and Development with Particular Reference to the African Revolution" heralds a philosophy with a pragmatic flavor, and Towa considers Nkrumah's the first attempt to conjoin philosophy with the struggle against domination. It is not rigor for rigor's sake that constitutes philosophy but rigor that has its foundations in the material conditions of the time, a rigor immersed in the past and present but with an eye toward the future. As we have already seen, Towa conceives of philosophy as a practice that moves beyond a preoccupation with ethnological considerations by calling into question the real relations of power in Africa. Only then does philosophy make itself relevant by taking a revolutionary role in social history.

A hermeneutical commitment of another kind is evident in Lansana Keita's classification. Keita disagrees with Towa's view that African philosophy began in 1970. Keita's classification, as we have seen, places the emphasis on writing and finds in Africa an old literary philosophical tradition. On Keita's view, then, the question about the existence of African philosophy can be resolved swiftly by pointing to the appropriate literature. The controversial aspect of Keita's commitment is the insistence that philosophy must be written, critical thought. Consequently, if the authorship of a text is questionable, or the texts in question cannot be produced in evidence, the claims of the existence of a philosophy are correspondingly weakened.

Keita is not alone in adopting this position about the importance of literacy. Paulin Hountondji defined African philosophy as the set of texts produced by Africans and called by their authors "philosophical." Such a definition obviously has many implications, one of which is that there does not exist a traditional African philosophy in the collective, unconscious myths of the people. Writing is the crucial determinant of whether philosophy exists. Embedded in this insistence on writing is the further controversy about whether the oral literatures of Africa are legitimate philosophical texts comparable to the written texts of Europe and the Western world. Here again, a commitment to a position on what constitutes a text shades seamlessly into a political critique. Whom is the notion produced for? Does it serve as another efficient means by which the African can be enslaved?

The Politics of Defining African Philosophy

The foregoing observations reveal that the question, Does African philosophy exist? is highly coded. It is not, as it first appears, an empirical question. It is a question that cannot be answered satisfactorily without an understanding of the often implicit ideological assumptions. The question further presupposes agreement on the issue of what constitutes philosophy. If the question of the existence of African philosophy is not an empirical one that can be answered by pointing to a literature, or even to African philosophers, what kind of question is it?

Disagreements about the meanings or origins of philosophy are not purely academic. An ongoing debate in America will illustrate this point. This is what has come to be known as the Bernal-Lefkowitz debate. Martin Bernal, professor of government studies at Cornell University, in his *Black Athena* makes a sustained effort to document "Greek cultural borrowings from Egypt and the Levant in the 2nd millennium BC or, to be more precise, in the thousand years from 2100 to 1100 BC."[62] Although Bernal does not claim, as other Afrocentrists after him have, that ancient Egyptians were black, the thrust of his argument is that the Afro-Asiatic influences of Classical civilization have vigorously and systematically been ignored, denied, or suppressed by Classicists. The reasons for that suppression range from guardianship of the status quo to racism. As Bernal says in the last sentence of his introduction to Vol. 1, "The political purpose of *Black Athena* is, of course, to lessen European cultural arrogance."[63] Afrocentrists are not all the same shade, as evidenced by the differences among Bernal and Molefi Asante, Maulana Karenga, and Leonard Jeffries. In different degrees, though, at the heart of their position is the view of Africa as the mother of Western civilization, the birthplace of science, mathematics, democracy, philosophy, and art.

Bernal's work is equally vigorously contested by Mary Lefkowitz, professor of classics at Wellesley College, who characterizes Afrocentrist teachings about antiquity as pseudohistory and myth. The "evidence" offered by the Afrocentrists for claiming that Greek civilization was derived from ancient Egypt lacks substance. In *Not out of Africa: How Afrocentrism Became an Excuse to Teach Myth as History*,[64] Lefkowitz challenges the revisionist histories, which as "theories are based on false assumptions and faulty reasoning, and cannot be supported by time-tested methods of intellectual inquiry."[65] Just as Bernal and others accuse the Lefkowitz side of cultural arrogance and racism, Lefkowitz and others accuse the Bernal side of no less than the political indoctrination of students. The accusations from both sides sometimes exceed the bounds of civility and pure scholarly exchange. When the debate is civil and scholarly, as in *Black Athena Revisited*,[66] classical scholars confront Bernal and other Afrocentric scholars on a wide range of issues such as whether ancient Egyptians could be considered black, whether there are ever good reasons to substitute myth for history, the interpretation of evidence, and most importantly, how to engage in exchanges of ideas on these difficult issues within a scholarly framework. To take a stand on any of these issues is to be engaged in the political.

Debate within African philosophy cannot be insulated from these wider issues. The long, dark days of colonialism link Africa to the West. It is tempting to imagine that debate conducted in dispassionate, objective tones. Indeed, in the popular mind there persists a view of the practice or discipline of philosophy as ahistorical, universal, and neutral. In the experience of Africa, however, definitions of philosophy have been peculiarly European. There is room for disagreement about whether it was by an accident of history or by design that philosophy came to be pressed into the service of Eurocentrism, sometimes explicitly, but mostly implicitly. European rationality came to claim universality. Although the roots of this claim go much further back, it was during the Renaissance and the Enlightenment that a European rationality began to claim universality. That claim played itself out in the explanation of reality, history, philosophy, and the world itself. That rationality is now associated with Western thought systems points to a great injustice. One consequence of that injustice has been the definition of Western rationality as the true discovery by the human mind of the essence of reality. This has meant the consignment of non-European rationalities and perspectives to the realm outside positive knowledge and in some cases even characterized as irrational. If by "non-European rationalities" one means the ways in which the production of knowledge is organized by non-Western cultures, the dilemma for the African philosopher is that philosophy ceased to be a tool empty in itself. Philosophy ceased, the moment European humanity began speaking on behalf of humanity in itself, to be a tool acquiring meaning only in its application to the observable world. Philosophy thus became the handmaiden of ideology in colonial Africa. In this highly partisan role, any view one takes about philosophy has far-reaching hegemonic implications. To deny the existence of African philosophy is to side with those discourses legitimating colonialism and marginalization. These discourses, by Africans and Europeans, devalue Africa while overvaluing Europe. In all cases they are systematic misrepresentations, ranging from the extremely crude views (from our contemporary vantage point) of Lucien Lévy-Bruhl about the primitive and inferior mentality of savage peoples,[67] through the "Bantu philosophy" supposedly uncovered by Tempels, to the "emotion is Negro as reason is Hellenic" of Senghor. Arguing for the existence of African philosophy thus becomes a contribution to the de-legitimating discourses against these perceived misrepresentations and their binary codes that pit primitive against civilized, savage against evolved, black against white, tradition against modernity, and Africa against Europe. It is to take sides against the imperialist domination of Africa. In the words of eminent Kenyan novelist Ngugi wa Thiong'o, philosophy ceases to be a tool of domination when it is deployed in the direction of "decolonizing the mind." Philosophy that does not help in this effort is seen as falling short of authenticity. It is on these grounds that philosophers with a hermeneutical orientation reject the ethnophilosophy of Tempels, Kagame, and Mbiti and the negritude of Senghor as contributions to African philosophy. It is that same problematic of authenticity, although a different interpretation of what constitutes authenticity, that would explain why Parker English, who gives Senghor a favorable reading, adopts a position so radically opposed to that of the hermeneutical philosophers.

Conclusion

Clearly, there is no easy answer to the question with which this chapter began. Defining African philosophy requires clarification of one's assumptions at different levels. That complex question, What is African philosophy to be defined as? requires that we understand, among other things: 1) what we are willing to count as philosophy in the strictest sense; 2) what we are willing to count as philosophical texts; 3) who is making the definition and for what audience (the question of motivations and intentions); and 4) one's ideological commitments.

The question has at once academic, psychological, historical, and ideological dimensions. Facile answers will not get to the bottom of it. It should come as no surprise that the debate about the definition and identity of African philosophy has gone on for so long. Excessive debate over identity, quite contrary to what some observers think, has not been unhealthy. Indeed, it was inescapable. In a larger sense, it is a debate about which philosophical works should be considered "canonical" and whether non-European perspectives can or should be accommodated within the traditional definitions of philosophy. Colonialism denied Africa an identity, disrupted society, and imposed European values. As a consequence, Africa is today a continent in which endemic poverty threatens to push the people deeper into hopelessness, while disease and illiteracy make the economic struggle for survival harder. One may well ask what these practical problems have to do with philosophy. Indeed, we may wonder why so much time and effort should be expended in debating different definitions of African philosophy when the continent is plagued with so many practical problems. A fitting response would be that the colonial experience made African identity acutely problematic. Although philosophers cannot now directly tackle the economic, social, and political problems, they can do their part in reclaiming African humanity by questioning how the traditional definitions of philosophy relate to politics. Thus, questions of Africanity are inextricably tied to these practical problems. Attempts to define African philosophy are therefore really attempts to clarify the mission of philosophy, and these attempts are meaningful only insofar as they are seen against the background of the larger picture I have attempted to paint in this chapter.

Study Questions

1. Although I have classified both Kwasi Wiredu and Paulin Hountondji as universalists (and Odera Oruka classifies them both as Professional philosophers), there are still differences in their definitions of African philosophy. What are these differences?

2. What are the difficulties of Hountondji's definition of African philosophy as "literature produced by Africans and described by them as philosophical"?

3. Do philosophers who take a hermeneutical approach to African philosophy find any value in African traditional beliefs and customs?

4. Take one ethnophilosopher and discuss the strengths or weaknesses of his definition of African philosophy.

5. Do you agree that defining African philosophy is an inherently political enterprise?

Notes

1. Placide Tempels, *La Philosophie Bantoue* (Elizabethville, Belgian Congo: Lovania, 1945). The second edition was published by Présence Africaine of Paris in 1949 and the third edition by the same publisher in 1965. The version to which I refer is *Bantu Philosophy*, trans. Rev. Colin King (Paris: Présence Africaine, 1959, 1969).

2. Tempels, *Bantu Philosophy*, 167.

3. Tempels, *Bantu Philosophy*, 40–1.

4. Tempels, *Bantu Philosophy*, 21.

5. Tempels, *Bantu Philosophy*, 167–8.

6. The idea of negritude pervades most of Senghor's writings but crystallizes in *Liberté I: Negritude et humanisme* (Paris: Seuil, 1964) and in *Les Fondements de l'africanité ou negritude et arabité* (Paris: Présence Africaine, 1967).

7. L. S. Senghor, *On African Socialism* (London: Pall Mall Press, 1964), 74.

8. Senghor, *On African Socialism*, 72.

9. Parker English, "On Senghor's Theory of Negritude," in *African Philosophy: A Classical Approach,* ed. Parker English and Kibujjo M. Kalumba (Upper Saddle River, N.J.: Prentice Hall, 1996), 57.

10. Innocent C. Onyewuenyi, "Is There an African Philosophy?" *Journal of African Studies* 3, no. 4 (1976–77): 513–28.

11. Campbell S. Momoh, "African Philosophy: Does It Exist?" *Diogenes (International Council for Philosophy and Humanistic Studies)* 130 (Summer 1985): 73–104.

12. Henri Maurier, "Do We Have an African Philosophy?" trans. Mildred M. McDevitt, in *African Philosophy: An Introduction,* ed. Richard A. Wright (Lanham, Md.: University Press of America, 1984), 25–40.

13. T. Carlos Jacques, "Is There an African Philosophy? The Politics of a

Question," *Sapina Bulletin: A Bulletin of the Society for African Philosophy in North America* 8, no. 1–2 (1995): 103–22.

14. Kwame Anthony Appiah, *In My Father's House: Africa in the Philosophy of Culture* (New York: Oxford University Press, 1992), 104.

15. Kwasi Wiredu, *Philosophy and an African Culture* (Cambridge: Cambridge University Press, 1980).

16. Wiredu, *Philosophy and an African Culture*, 39.

17. Wiredu, *Philosophy and an African Culture*, 42–3.

18. Ali A. Mazrui and Toby Kleban Levine, eds., *The Africans: A Reader* (New York: Praeger, 1986), xv.

19. Kwasi Wiredu, "Morality and Religion in Akan Thought," in *Philosophy and Cultures: Proceedings of the Second Afro-Asian Philosophy Conference, Nairobi, October/November 1981*, ed. H. Odera Oruka and D.A. Masolo (Nairobi: Bookwise, 1983), 6–13; Also see his *Philosophy and an African Culture* (Cambridge: Cambridge University Press, 1980). Other examples of Wiredu's characteristic approach to philosophy can be seen in his "African Philosophical Tradition: A Case Study of the Akan," *The Philosophical Forum* 24, no. 1–3 (1992–93): 35–62; and in "The African Concept of Personhood," in *African-American Perspectives on Biomedical Ethics*, ed. Harley E. Flack and Edmund D. Pellegrino (Washington, D.C.: Georgetown University Press, 1992), 104–17.

20. Kwasi Wiredu, "On Defining African Philosophy," in *African Philosophy: The Essential Readings*, ed. Tsenay Serequeberhan (New York: Paragon House, 1991), 105.

21. Paulin Hountondji, "Reason and Tradition," in *Philosophy and Cultures: Proceedings of the Second Afro-Asian Philosophy Conference, Nairobi, October/November 1981*, ed. H. Odera Oruka and D. A. Masolo (Nairobi: Bookwise, 1983), 136–7.

22. Paulin Hountondji, "African Philosophy: Myth and Reality" in *African Philosophy: The Essential Readings*, ed. Tsenay Serequeberhan (New York: Paragon House, 1991), 118–9.

23. Hountondji, "Myth and Reality," 120.

24. Hountondji, "Myth and Reality," 120.

25. Paulin Hountondji, *African Philosophy: Myth and Reality*, second ed. (Bloomington: Indiana University Press, 1996).

26. Henry Odera Oruka, ed., *Sage Philosophy: Indigenous Thinkers and Modern Debate on African Philosophy* (Leiden: E. J. Brill, 1990).

27. Henry Odera Oruka, "Sagacity in African Philosophy," in *African Philosophy: The Essential Readings*, ed. Tsenay Serequeberhan (New York: Paragon House, 1991), 52.

28. Odera Oruka, "Sagacity in African Philosophy," 52.

29. Jay M. van Hook, "Kenyan Sage Philosophy: A Review and Critique," *The Philosophical Forum* 27, no. 1 (1995): 54–65.

30. Anke Graness and Kai Kresse, eds., *Sagacious Reasoning: Henry Odera Oruka in Memoriam* (Frankfurt: Peter Lang, 1997).

31. Tsenay Serequeberhan, ed., *African Philosophy: The Essential Readings* (New York: Paragon House, 1991).

32. Serequeberhan, *African Philosophy*, 22–3.

33. Tsenay Serequeberhan, *The Hermeneutics of African Philosophy: Horizon and Discourse* (New York: Routledge, 1994).

34. Serequeberhan, *The Hermeneutics of African Philosophy*, 85.

35. Serequeberhan, *The Hermeneutics of African Philosophy*, 117–8.

36. Serequeberhan, *The Hermeneutics of African Philosophy*, 78.

37. Marcien Towa, *Essai sur la problematique philosophique dans l'Afrique actuelle* (Yaounde, Cameroon: Editions Clé, 1971).

38. Marcien Towa, "Conditions for the Affirmation of a Modern Philosophical Thought," in *African Philosophy: The Essential Readings*, ed. Tsenay Serequeberhan (New York: Paragon House, 1991), 195.

39. Towa, "Conditions for Affirmation," 197.

40. Towa, "Conditions for Affirmation," 197.

41. Okonda Okolo, "Tradition and Destiny: Horizons of an African Philosophical Hermeneutics," in *African Philosophy: The Essential Readings*, ed. Tsenay Serequeberhan (New York: Paragon House, 1991), 201–9.

42. Theophilus Okere, "*Can There Be an African Philosophy? A Hermeneutical Investigation with Special Reference to Igbo Culture*," (Ph.D. diss., Louvain University, 1971).

43. Nkombe Oleko, "*Métaphore et métonymie dans les symboles paremiologiques tetela*," (Ph.D. diss., Louvain University, 1975).

44. Okolo, "Tradition and Destiny," 204.

45. Okolo, "Tradition and Destiny," 206.

46. Cheikh Anta Diop, *Precolonial Black Africa*, trans. Harold Salemson (Westport, Conn.: Lawrence Hill, 1987).

47. Kwame Nkrumah, *Consciencism* (New York: Monthly Review Press, 1970), 79.

48. Peter Bodunrin, "The Question of African Philosophy," *Philosophy* 56, no. 216 (1981): 162–79.

49. Kwame Gyekye, *An Essay on African Philosophical Thought: The Akan Conceptual Scheme*, rev. ed. (Philadelphia: Temple University Press, 1995).

50. Innocent Onyewuenyi, "Is There an African Philosophy?" *Journal of African Studies* 3, no. 4 (1976–77): 513–28.

51. Frantz Fanon, *Les Damnés de la Terre* (Paris: Présence Africaine, 1963, 1991).

52. Lucius Outlaw, "African Philosophy: Deconstructive and Reconstructive Challenges," in *Contemporary Philosophy: African Philosophy*, ed. Guttorm Floistad (Boston: Martinus Nijhoff, 1987), 11–19.

53. Lucius Outlaw, "African, African American, Africana Philosophy," *The Philosophical Forum* 24, no. 1–3 (1992–93): 63–93.

54. V. Y. Mudimbe, *The Invention of Africa: Gnosis, Philosophy, and the Order of Knowledge* (Bloomington: Indiana University Press, 1988).

55. Henry Odera Oruka, "Four Trends in Current African Philosophy," paper presented at the William Amo Symposium in Accra, Ghana, July 24–29, 1978. See also his *Sage Philosophy*, 1–10.

56. Henry Odera Oruka, *Sage Philosophy: Indigenous Thinkers and Modern Debate on African Philosophy* (Leiden: E. J. Brill, 1990).

57. Lansana Keita, "Contemporary African Philosophy: The Search for a Method," *Praxis International* 5, no. 2 (July 1985): 145–61.

58. Keita, "Contemporary African Philosophy," 155.

59. Keita, "Contemporary African Philosophy," 156.

60. Lansana Keita, "The African Philosophical Tradition," in *African Philosophy: An Introduction*, ed. Richard Wright (Lanham, Md.: University Press of America, 1984), 57–76.

61. Keita, "The African Philosophical Tradition," 70.

62. Martin Bernal, *Black Athena: The Afroasiatic Roots of Classical Civilization, Vol 1: The Fabrication of Ancient Greece 1785–1985* (New Brunswick, N.J.: Rutgers University Press, 1987), 17.

63. Bernal, *Black Athena, Vol 1,* 73.

64. Mary Lefkowitz, *Not out of Africa: How Afrocentrism Became an Excuse to Teach Myth as History* (New York: Basic Books, 1996).

65. Lefkowitz, *Not out of Africa*, xiii.

66. Mary Lefkowitz and Guy MacLean Rogers, eds., *Black Athena Revisited* (Chapel Hill: University of North Carolina Press, 1996).

67. Lucien Lévy-Bruhl, *How Natives Think* (Princeton: Princeton University Press, 1986).

PART TWO

Ethnophilosophy
and
Its Critics

◙

Is Ethnophilosophy
Really
Philosophy?

◙

Defining ethnophilosophy is a complicated business, if only because no African philosopher willingly admits to being called an ethnophilosopher. "Ethnophilosophy" is a term coined by opponents of the group of poets, philosophers, and anthropologists who look for African philosophy in the cultures of the different peoples. Ethnophilosophers are to African philosophy what the Sophists were to classical Greek philosophers. The Sophists were not, technically, philosophers. Their opponents claimed that they taught any subject whatever for which there was a popular demand. Protagoras undertook to impart to his pupils the principles of success as a politician or as a private citizen. Gorgias taught rhetoric and politics, Hippias history, mathematics, and physics.

Likening ethnophilosophers such as Tempels, Kagame, and Senghor to Sophists such as Protagoras, Gorgias, and Hippias is bound to strike some readers as odd. I do not mean that ethnophilosophers make purely rhetorical arguments such as the Sophists were accused of. Nor is the comparison meant to portray ethnophilosophers as skillful manipulators of language who would attempt to make the worse argument appear the better. What I want the comparison to focus on is the pejorative connotation that attaches to both "Sophist" and "ethnophilosopher." The similarities lie in the negative connotations that come from being defined by one's opponents. Indeed, the appellation "ethnophilosophy" is something of an insult, because to be an ethnophilosopher is to be seen by universalist philosophers to purport to practice philosophy in a manner that deviates from the conventional. From Paulin Hountondji, one of the fiercest critics of ethnophilosophy, we get a sense of what "conventional philosophy" is. In the usual meaning of the word "philosophy," there is a sense of a system of thought constructed by individual authors. Philosophy reflects the expression of personal interpretations rather than the collective thought of "Africans" or "Bantu" in general. The disciples of Tempels and the negritude poets begin by describing the collective values of a people. Then, without warning, they switch to a defense and reclamation of these values. This is not, however, how conventional philosophy proceeds. Philosophy would first attempt to justify the values to be reclaimed.

Hountondji situates ethnophilosophy within a larger framework of similar practices in the literature:

> ethnobotany, ethnozoology, ethnobiology, ethnopsychiatry, ethnomedicine, ethnominerology, ethnopsychoanalysis, ethnopsychology, ethnomusicology, ethnolinguistics, ethnomethodology, ethno-history, ethnosociology, ethnotypology, ethnodemographics, ethnotechnology, and even ethno-epistemology and ethnocuisine all being terms that respectively designate either disciplines being constituted, of emerging theoretical project.[1]

All ethno- projects share theoretical, methodological, and ideological presuppositions. Hountondji thus uses the word "ethnophilosophy":

> to designate the same type of analysis by placing into question not only the confusion of methods but also the status of the object that one is attempting to restore: the "African philosophy," the so-called primitive philosophy, understood as a system of collective thought, spontaneous, implicit, inalterable, to which all the members of a given society would adhere. In my opinion, such a hypothesis seemed to translate a unanimous prejudice, a prejudice according to which everyone would agree on everything in societies of this type.[2]

Hountondji's characterization of ethnophilosophy was discussed in Chapter 1. It is important, however, to repeat here the features of ethnophilosophy so that it is clear exactly why I classify Tempels, Kagame, and Mbiti together with Diop, Senghor, and Ogotemmeli. The core of ethnophilosophy is its function as a descriptive anthropology. In contrast to a discursive, analytical philosophy, ethnophilosophy treats as philosophy the indigenous cosmologies, the traditional beliefs such as those about supernatural beings and magic. Beliefs, myths, and cosmology are believed to be interwoven into the complex ritual practices that are the manifestation of philosophy. Unwritten and unsystematized, the rituals and systems of belief nevertheless form an intricate web that guides the people in making sense of their lives. Through a description of the rituals and beliefs, the cosmology and religious worldview of the people can be reconstructed. Each member of the community cannot be expected to reproduce, on request, an overarching philosophy, a framework within which he or she organizes the totality of his or her experience. That framework can be extracted from the art, the ways in which communication is structured, the agricultural practices, and the music. The languages and oral traditions reveal legends and proverbs about the culture, morality, religion, and history. In these myths, folk tales, and proverbs, one learns the place of the individual in the world. In a number of the Bantu languages of East, Central, and Southern Africa, proverbs reveal the collective, socializing, and participatory emphasis of the culture. The emphasis is on personhood in the social context. The Sotho say, "*Motho ke motho ka batho*," and the Xhosa, "*Umuntu ngumuntu ngabantu*," meaning "Man is man by his fellowmen." The same idea surfaces in the Kiswahili saying "*Kidole kimoja hakiui chawa* (A single finger does not kill lice)." The idea is that the individual is meaningless in isolation and makes sense only as part of the totality.

The metaphysical conviction of a mutual belonging together exhibits itself in other ways, for example, in opinions and practices about the extended family. In those practices there is detectable a collective, unconscious idea that the community has the duty to help or let individuals share in the wealth generated within the communities of which they are integral parts. This idea may involve great frustration for some individuals. From the standpoint of ethics, group interests are seen as having precedence over individual autonomy. Given the high level of communal attachment, the most outstanding wrongs are therefore sins against the group. The morality of acts of commission or omission can be truly gauged only when one understands the cosmology within which they are committed. It is a cosmology that emphasizes the social dimension of life—an emphasis that reveals itself in another way that is particularly pertinent to the discussion about philosophy. Ethnophilosophy explains the absence of individual philosophers by pointing to a rich heritage in which individuals gain respect and prominence in the measure to which they identify with the group. Where individuals do not look for their own glory, it is inappropriate to look for philosophy in the sense of a personalized, critical literature.

These are the general principles of ethnophilosophy. In discussing ethnophilosophy I gave specific examples of authors whose works fall under these general principles—Tempels, Kagame, Senghor, Nyerere, and Nkrumah. In this chapter we explore some of these works in more detail and introduce others. The sense that should come out of this chapter is that there are many brands of ethnophilosophy. We begin the examination of these different brands with the work of Cheikh Anta Diop.

Cheikh Anta Diop: An Afrocentric Historiography

A Senegalese man of letters, Cheikh Anta Diop (1923–1986) is not one who would immediately be considered an ethnophilosopher—thanks to the complex nature of his scholarship. Here I want to follow Albert Mosley, who in his anthology *African Philosophy: Selected Readings*³ correctly recognizes the ethnophilosophical features of Diop's work. Diop assumes a high level of unity between the different traditional African cosmologies. His arguments for African civilization are made within a metaphysical and epistemological framework that presumes an essential unity among the different African cultures. Such a unity among cultures is, of course, one of the central principles of ethnophilosophy. His acceptance of this principle does not, however, commit him to the further step of accepting negritude. In *Nations nègres et culture*,⁴ Diop disagrees with the negritude poets and philosophers who deny reason and reflective thought to the Negro African. In opposition to aspects of the negritude movement, Diop argues for a technologically advanced traditional Africa. To counter the claims made by Europeans about the lack of technological advancement in precolonial Africa, he writes about Africa as a distinctive land mass comparable to Europe in many respects, yet one whose historical, political, and religious wealth has remained a mystery to Western observers because of the way the continent's history has been presented to them. Here is how Diop begins his *Precolonial Black Africa*:

> One thereby understands the technical and other lags to be the result of a different kind of development based upon absolutely objective fundamental causes.

Thus, there is no longer any reason for embarrassment.

Once this awareness achieved, we can immediately and fully in almost every slightest detail relive all the aspects of African national life: the administrative, judicial, economic, and military organizations, that of labor, the technical level, the migrations and formations of peoples and nationalities, thus their ethnic genesis, and consequently almost linguistic genesis, etc.

Upon absorbing any such human experience, we sense deep within ourselves a true reinforcement of our feeling of cultural oneness.[5]

In this passage, Diop has set up the classic ethnophilosophical project. Three components of the project—the motivation, the sources to be excavated, and unity of cultures—are the points of departure. The motivation is to furnish an antithesis to European scholarship on at least two levels: to reclaim the dignity of the African by responding to the European denigration of Africans' achievements, and to reclaim the Africanity and blackness of the ancient Egyptians. Diop speculates, based on available documents on African history, that ancient Greek scientists and philosophers learned much of that science and philosophy from Egypt. This line of inquiry he pioneers is then later developed more vigorously by subsequent Afrocentrists such as Maulana Karenga and Molefi Asante. In a crucial sense, then, Diop's approach is similar to that of the European scholars he challenges. He uses his multidisciplinary skills to locate the foundations of Africa's cultural and intellectual civilizations in ancient Egypt just as European scholars had located the foundations of European civilization in ancient Greece. In so doing he provides the foundations of an African historiography of which Africans no longer need be embarrassed. Diop's searching gaze goes beyond any traditional academic discipline, and since he is not constrained by the usual limitations of the specific disciplines, his method allows the freedom to incorporate evidence from diverse sources. In that evidence Diop sees the high quality of ancient Egyptian civilization, which must once again be brought to the notice of Western observers to make the twin points that this civilization began in Africa, and further that it played a crucial role in the formation of ancient Greek civilization. The interdisciplinary method Diop employs takes as a key premise the view that the philosophy or philosophies of a culture cannot be found in any explicitly expressed form but rather by looking at the various aspects of cultural life.

By looking at the aspects of cultural life Diop lists, such as administrative, judicial, economic, military, and so on, one reaches an understanding of the philosophical system. With an understanding of the philosophical system comes the reinforcement of the feeling that despite the internal multiplicity of African cultures there is nonetheless an underlying continental cultural oneness. The cultural oneness is a result of the "absolutely objective fundamental causes" Diop refers to in the preface to *Precolonial Black Africa*. Europe and Africa are qualitatively different and produce corresponding epistemological frameworks that are fundamentally distinct and yet equally valuable.

We could make this point using two examples—the concept of caste and the political organization of the old empires of Ghana, Mali, and Songhai. For the concept of caste, Diop analyzes his native Senegal but states that the conclusions drawn hold true for "the whole of detribalized Sudanese Africa." He writes:

> It seems necessary at the outset to point out the specific features of the caste system, in order more clearly to bring out the difference in social structure which has always existed between Europe and Africa. The originality of the system resides in the fact that the dynamic elements of society, whose discontent might have engendered revolution, are really satisfied with their social condition and do not seek to change it. . . . In Africa, it is not rare for members of the lower caste to refuse to enter into conjugal relations with those of the higher caste, even though the reverse would seem more normal.[6]

Diop is here stressing the difference of African socioeconomic structures from those of Europe. Each structure must be viewed from a perspective that recognizes its radically different particularity. Reciprocity in such an outlook does not allow the treatment of any structure as a deviation from the standard. Thus, respect and tolerance are fostered between cultures of the world as they attempt to cope with their environments. The caste system then, for example, develops according to the accidents of history. There are not any general laws guiding the development of the concept in Europe and Africa. The African of lower caste who passes up opportunities to join a higher caste must be understood in terms of his or her social structure. European disrespect of and hostility toward Africa derives from a failure to understand African social frameworks. Different social structures make possible different forms of adaptation to unique situations.

Another example Diop employs to illustrate this point is the process by which societies move from feudal to capitalistic production. Europe, India, China, Japan, and precolonial Africa did not go through identical transformations during corresponding periods in their economies. If there were general principles guiding the way in which societies evolve from one mode of production to another, then we should expect all societies to go through similar processes at comparable stages of their evolution. The evidence, however, has not shown anything of the sort. This lack of evidence of a natural law holding for all societies is for Diop evidence that modern capitalism in these other societies is a contagious European virus that infects these societies at the moment of contact with Europe.

Diop makes the same argument about different social structures by using the examples of Ghana, Mali, and Songhai. These ancient kingdoms were governed in ways unknown in the Europe of the time:

> With Charlemagne commenced the first effort at centralization; but one can say without exaggeration that throughout the Middle Ages Europe never found a form of political organization superior to that of African states. There is agreement on the fact that the African variety of organization is indigenous: it could not have come from the Aryan or Semitic Mediterranean. If one absolutely had to relate it to some earlier forms, the administrative centralization of Pharaonic Egypt, with its *nomes*, might be brought up.[7]

A tension is evident in the work of Diop. He recognizes the multiplicity of cultures and social structures—and the originality and particularity of their cosmologies. Each makes its unique intellectual contribution. Diop is not locked into these particularities, however. He envisions communication between these various radically different particularisms. Yet in the manner of Western scholars before him, he identifies with his own culture as the originator of world civilization. His procedure is reminiscent of Eurocentric writings that considered a particular kind of reason to be the universal and most genuine expression of humanity and considered non-European rationalities as deviating from that standard. His purpose, though, is to declare intellectual independence from Europe. Given the foregoing, it should be clearer why the work of Diop has eagerly been appropriated by latter-day Afrocentrists of all shades. It is only an independent Africa, one not distinguished only by its exotism to ethnologists, that can engage in a dialogue and communication necessitated by the interdependence among cultures. Indeed, in *Civilization or Barbarism*[8] Diop turns the tables on Europe, which has always described itself as civilized. It is here that Diop gives his most developed account of Egyptian philosophy and of the impact of Egyptian ideas on an ungrateful Europe that still fails to acknowledge the profound impact of Egyptian ideas. When the ancient Egyptians were developing their ideas, Europe was still barbaric. But this barbarism need not continue in its present form of denying the importance of African intellectual contributions.

John S. Mbiti: A Religious Ethnography

Kenyan theologian John S. Mbiti (1931–   ) takes an approach that is ethnophilosophical in a straightforward sense. To illustrate difference between Europe and Africa, and to prove his claim of cultural specificity, he uses an ethnic or ethnographical approach that studies specific peoples of Africa (say, the Akamba ethnic group of Kenya). Though he begins with an interest in specific African ethnic groups, Mbiti's is not an approach aiming for cultural rejuvenation. He looks within the social and cultural environments of the African people to discover ways in which the Christian faith may be made clearer and comprehensible to Africans. It is therefore a procedure that seeks to understand and interpret Christianity in the light of the African condition—essentially an Africanization of Christianity.

Mbiti's approach does not doubt the existence of an African philosophy within the traditional cultures. The wisdom of African people nonetheless cannot be compartmentalized into tidy, identifiable categories. The existence of philosophy is beyond contestation. The philosophy is disclosed in the history and culture of the people, and it is that African cultural background that must be the point of departure for elaborating or constructing its framework. Africans themselves do not need a specialized discipline labeled "philosophy," because philosophy is inseparable from their everyday actions and ways of being.

Mbiti, like Diop, operates within a scheme that assumes a linguistic, religious, and cultural unity of the African continent. Africans are profoundly and universally religious. Since every action is religious, no specialized discipline of religion is necessary. We may thus understand why Mbiti consistently conjoins "African religions and philosophy." The symbolic acts of initiation into a social class, sacrifice of an animal, and pouring libations to the ancestors are all actions through which people understand themselves and their place within the culture. Further, these symbolic actions reveal the categories operative in the culture and point to the ways in which the culture integrates the physical world with the mythical and spiritual. Lessons in African ontology are contained in the ritual actions, and indeed in the actions of day-to-day existence. Mbiti is aware of the European scholarship that, without understanding African ways, has characterized Africans who revere a particular tree as fetishists, and those who sacrifice animals to appease the spirits of their ancestors as animists. Mbiti says:

> because traditional religions permeate all the departments of life, there is no formal distinction between the sacred and the secular, between the religious and the non-religious, between the spiritual and the material areas of life. Wherever the African is, there is his religion: he carries it to the field where he is sowing seeds or harvesting a new crop; he takes it with him to the beer party or to attend a funeral ceremony. . . .[9]

Thus, the tree is revered not as a specialized edifice for worship but because of its symbolic strength, longevity, and stability. Libation and animal sacrifice are not evidence of ancestor worship, but symbolic reaffirmation of personhood by renewing the religious relationship with other persons, living and dead.

Africans therefore utilize a different ontology from that of Europeans. It is an ontology, as he says, according to which the African is in deep and intimate worship in his or her every action. Personhood depends on relationship with other persons, hence the importance of ancestors and spirits in the cosmological scheme. Unlike in the West, individuals are not automatically conferred with personhood by virtue of existing in society. Only by the decision of other human beings does one become a human being. Within this ontology Mbiti excavates the basic features of African philosophy on such issues as the concept of time, death and immortality, the living and the dead, and magic and witchcraft. Of all these issues, Mbiti's most controversial theme is his exposition of the African concept of time.

From his ethnocultural observations of the Akamba of Kenya, and from a linguistic comparison of Akamba, Gikuyu, and English verb tenses, Mbiti concludes that Africans distinguish two types of time. He designates these using the Kiswahili words *Sasa* and *Zamani*:

> according to traditional concepts, time is a two-dimensional phenomenon, with a long *past*, a *present*, and virtually *no future*. The linear concept of time in Western thought, with an indefinite past, present and indefinite future, is practically foreign to African thinking. The future is virtually absent because events which lie in it have not taken place, they have not been realized and cannot, therefore constitute time. . . . *Actual time* is therefore what is present and what is past. It moves "backward" rather than "forward"; and people set their minds not on future things but chiefly in what has taken place.[10]

Sasa is the dimension of time consisting of the present, the experienced past, and a very short future. It is measured by the main social activities of the individual and the group. The second type of time is *Zamani*. Everything comes from and ends in *Zamani*:

> *Zamani* overlaps with *Sasa* and the two are not separable. Sasa feeds or disappears into *Zamani*. But before events become incorporated into the *Zamani*, they have to become realized or actualized within the *Sasa* dimension. When this has taken place, then the events 'move' backwards from the *Sasa* into the *Zamani*. So *Zamani* becomes the period beyond which nothing can go. *Zamani* is the graveyard of time, the period of termination, the dimension in which everything finds its halting point.[11]

The twin dimensions of *Sasa* and *Zamani* leave no room for the future as actual time. The faraway future does not exist. An infinite future beyond two years is unthinkable. Mbiti uses the myths of African peoples as examples of how they think about time. All African peoples have creation myths and fables about the *Zamani*, though these myths differ in their details as they are told by the different ethnic groups. The Shilluk of Sudan, Ewe of Togo, and Efe of Zaire believe God made human beings from the earth (different colors for different folks). The Pangwe of Cameroon hold that human beings started life as tailless, lizardlike creatures in the water. There are myths about the creation of man and woman, of good and bad people, of different ethnic and racial groups. What Mbiti finds interesting is the absence, with one or two possible exceptions, among African people of apocalyptic myths or doomsday scenarios. Mbiti interprets the absence of "end of the world" myths to mean African time is cyclical, the history of its measure depending on the social activities of the group under consideration. Past events return eternally in the memories and actions of the living. Africans reckon time through their webs of interaction rather than by dividing it into years, months, or seasons.

A uniquely African ontology is nestled between the *Zamani* and the *Sasa*. It is a hierarchical ontology composed of the following categories:

- God
- Spirits
- Human beings
- Animals and plants
- Phenomena and objects

This is an anthropocentric ontology that places humans at the center of the universe. Although human beings are in constant relation with God, who is the creator of all things, they do not need to develop a special theology or specialized shrines and monuments expressly for worship. The ancestors, both the long-departed spirits and the more recently departed "living dead" bridge the gap between life and death, providing the glue that holds together the traditions of the group. Humans stand in religious relations with God, spirits, animals, and plants, indeed with the natural elements earth, water, air, and fire. The whole of existence is a deeply religious phenomenon.

We must remember that Mbiti is writing as an African Christian. As an African he emphasizes the *difference* of African culture to highlight the "ignorance, prejudice and falsifications" of which Western scholarship has been guilty. He is concerned to counteract the myths of the African as a savage incapable of religious sentiment, together with the myths about human and animal sacrifice. Mbiti is convinced that Africans are deeply religious. Yet as a Christian he sees his mission as assimilating this unique African universe, with its deep religiosity, to the message of Christianity. The way he negotiates between these two roles raises fundamental questions that leave him open to criticism by the critics of ethnophilosophy. Philosophers who take the hermeneutical approach denounce Mbiti's proselytizing as nothing short of an attempt to enslave

Africans anew to foreign gods—an attempt all the more dangerous owing to Mbiti's understanding of traditional African beliefs and customs. Universalists remain uncomfortable with Mbiti's reliance on communal worldviews and his equation of these with philosophy.

Ogotemmeli's Cosmology

A common criticism of ethnophilosophy is that it heralds a philosophy without philosophers. The sage Ogotemmeli of the Dogon people of southern Mali presents an exposition of Dogon mythological thinking that puts this criticism in a new light. In a sense Ogotemmeli may be considered an absent philosopher because he died long before he became aware of his notoriety as a philosopher. If he was a philosopher, he was not aware of it. In another sense, however, there are those who doubt that Ogotemmeli's exposition, however systematic, amounts to philosophy. On this view it can, at best, be read as an expression of collective, unconscious myths and a knowledge of Dogon social and cultural features. Even if one admits that Ogotemmeli is a philosopher, his exposition of Dogon culture still does not qualify as philosophy.

Doubts of a different kind are raised by those within Griaule's anthropological circles who question the authenticity and accuracy of the worldview attributed to the Dogon sage. It is too systematic, too Pan-African in its outlook, and too foreign in its categories. This last criticism amounts to saying that the Ogotemmeli–Griaule connection is a case of the blind leading the blind (the allusion here is to Ogotemmeli's physical blindness and Griaule's conceptual blindness about what constitutes philosophy).

The whole controversy began innocuously enough. Here are the uncontroversial facts. French ethnologist Marcel Griaule and Ogotemmeli held conversations for thirty-three days in 1933. The informant conversed on Dogon beliefs and myths about the origins of the world, and traditions relating to Dogon history, ontology, culture, and society. Griaule published the "report of Ogotemmeli's teaching" in 1948.[12] Here is where the difficulties begin. It is unclear whether Griaule was reporting a monologue or a dialogue. There was skepticism about how the uneducated (in Western ways, that is) Ogotemmeli could exhibit such an apparently comprehensive knowledge of the connections between Dogon social organization and its images, symbols, and cosmology and the cosmic universe. Griaule himself acknowledges an affinity between his method and that of Placide Tempels—an acknowledgment that raises fears that he, perhaps unconsciously, systematized and synthesized Ogotemmeli's reports of the myths into an organized metaphysics. What are we to make of these connections? Griaule explicitly puts his work in the tradition of Tempels:

> Ten years ago [G. Dieterlen's *Les Ames des Dogon* (1941), S. de Ganay's *Les Devises* (1941), and my own *Les Masques* (1938)] had already drawn attention to new facts concerning the "vital force". . . . They have shown the primary importance of the notion of the person and his relations with society, with the universe, and with the divine. Thus Dogon ontology has opened new vistas for ethnologist. . . . More recently . . . the Rev. Fr. Tempels presented an analysis of conception of this kind, and raised the question of whether Bantu thought should not be regarded as a system of philosophy.[13]

At the very least, it is clear from this that Griaule is operating within a framework that sees connections between the ontologies of the Bantu and the Dogon. The importance of the concept of vital force, indeed the universal interaction of forces, establishes an affinity between Dogon and Bantu. We can only wonder what other parts of the "Conversations" are systematizations in this manner.

Force ontology aside, let us consider what can be made of the substance of some of Ogotemmeli's teachings. A number of general principles are embedded in his retelling of the main Dogon myth, the myth of creation. *Amma*, the god of heaven, in the manner of a potter first created the sun from white-hot clay. From clay at a lower temperature *Amma* fashioned the moon. Later, *Amma* created black people from sunlight and white people from moonlight. The earth is a lump of clay, the stars pellets of earth. *Amma* made the earth in the shape of a female body, the femaleness represented by a receptive ant hill. Interacting with the force he had created, *Amma* had sexual intercourse with the earth. The first animal, the Golden Jackal, was born.

Amma continued his interaction with the earth, fertilizing it a second time by means of rain. Two identical beings, twins half human but with tails and forked tongues like green snakes were born:

> The pair were born perfect and complete; they had eight members and their number was eight, which is the symbol of speech. They were also of the essence of God, since they

were made of his seed which is at once the ground, the form
and the substance of the life-force of the world, from which
derives the motion and the persistence of created being. This
force is water, and the pair are present in all water: they ARE
water. . . .[14]

The identical twins—the *Nommo* (water)—contained within them
the essence of water of fertility (their green color), and of men and
serpents. They are linked both to the earth and to the sky. The *Nommo*
together became vegetation. Leaving the grass, plants, and trees on earth,
they joined their father *Amma* in heaven. From their vantage point in
the sky, the *Nommo* spy the nakedness of mother earth. Introducing their
own interaction with the earth, they bring to earth ten types of fibers,
divided in two groups, to cover the ant hill (genitalia) of their mother.
The movement of the twins stirs up a wind that in turn moves the leaves
and branches. This is the start of language on earth. Just as the wind
wove the reeds and shrubs to clothe naked mother earth, so too did
language creation clothe human speechlessness. "There was recreated by
human lips the concept of life in motion, of the transposition of forces,
of the efficacity of the breath of the spirit. . . ."[15] Language is a form of
weaving. Speech clothes humans just as vegetation clothed the earth. To
be naked is to be speechless.

Language is important for another reason. As Griaule writes, "What
makes life is not so much force but the movement of forces."[16] The
central importance of the word is that it affects the life force of other
beings. We may see in Ogotemmeli's account a vision of the word as
regenerative and restorative (whether Ogotemmeli made this connection is a quite a different matter). This point, I think, anticipates the
discussion of the relationship between language and philosophy, which
we should defer for the moment.

But we are getting ahead of the story. Before human language could
develop, human beings had to be created. *Amma* created the first man
and woman out of the earth's clay and gave them life—*Nyama*. *Nyama*
is the soul and vital principle with which everything is endowed. *Amma*
then circumcised both man and woman. The excised skin from the man
became a black and white lizard. The clitoridectomy resulted in a scor-
pion. The sexual union of the first couple produces four sets of twins—
four boys followed by four girls. These sets of twins are the ancestors of
the eight Dogon families. The ancestors then disappeared into the earth
and, guided by the *Nommo*, the male *Nommo* returned as a fetus to the

womb of the female *Nommo*. And thus the processes of re-creation, re-generation, and restoration.

The reader who wishes to delve deeper into an analysis of Ogotemmeli's cosmogony is invited to peruse the excellent treatment by Dismas A. Masolo[17] and the review of *Conversations with Ogotemmeli* by J. Goody.[18] The features of Dogon ontology to which I have drawn attention in this brief sketch are:

1. The explicit assertion by Griaule of the principle of vital force as a point of affinity between Dogon cosmology and Bantu (Baluba) cosmology. Interaction of forces underlies the very similar ways in which these different peoples apprehend their reality and also their forms of expression.

2. The various stages of the creation myth as told by Ogotemmeli. The main stages whose meanings we must seek to learn (and that Griaule should have pushed Ogotemmeli to elaborate on or analyze) are:

- Creation of sun, moon, earth, and stars
- Birth of the Jackal
- Coming of the twins *Nommo*
- *Nommo* covering the nakedness of the earth
- Creation of the first man and woman
- Appearance of eight ancestors of the Dogon
- Ancestors' disappearance into the earth
- Ancestors' retiring to heaven
- Heaven's granary stolen and returned to earth by one of the eight ancestors

3. The hierarchical order of the Dogon cosmic and social order. Creative force is more active than created force. Every force continues to interact with forces it has created. Through the creation in several stages the world is structurally ordered, with everything in its place.

4. The concepts of *Nommo* and *Nyama*. The constant and universal interaction of forces saps the force of individual existents. *Nommo* therefore is constantly preoccupied with restoring and regenerating *Nyama*—the vital principle of existing beings.

Ogotemmeli outlines in detail over the thirty-three days an extremely intricate Dogon cosmology, one that links earthly things to heavenly ones. The celestial granary that is the object of that struggle during creation is described thus: "The granary and all it contained was therefore a picture of the world system of the new order, and the way this system worked was represented by the functioning of the internal organs."[19] Throughout the thirty-three days of the "conversations," Ogotemmeli talks in this vein. Is this philosophy? When pressed, Ogotemmeli explains the analogies he employs by recourse to even more oblique symbolic language. This is without doubt a systematic ethnophilosophy. Ogotemmeli therefore easily qualifies as what Odera Oruka has characterized as a folk sage. But does his systematic ethnophilosophy achieve the status of philosophy? Critics of ethnophilosophy offer a number of arguments that challenge the equation of ethnophilosophy, even a systematic ethnophilosophy, with philosophy.

The Critics of Ethnophilosophy

The methods and claims of ethnophilosophy have been questioned from many quarters. Critics at one extreme treat ethnophilosophy as a dangerous irrelevancy, a clinging to outmoded traditional belief systems in a modern world. At the most charitable extreme are the critics who consider a description of these belief systems a useful *beginning* for the philosophical enterprise of rational inquiry. Between these extremes there are middle positions that take issue with particular methodological mistakes, or specific implications of ethnophilosophical claims.

I begin this survey of the critics of ethnophilosophy with feminist critiques—an often-ignored dimension in the discussions within African philosophy. The traditional African belief systems so dear to ethnophilosophers ignore the structures in African societies that oppress and marginalize women. To uncritically accept those belief systems is to take an approach that ignores the experience of women in patriarchal and male-dominated societies. In societies that have been dominated by men, dehumanizing and oppressive customs, taboos, and traditions are the "normal" cultural elements. African women have always suffered from these patriarchal structures. For example, behind most of the parables, proverbs, and myths, there is the wish to dominate women. The creation myths from all over the continent have women coming into creation long after men (for examples, the myths of the Ewe of Togo, Efe of Zaire, and Nandi of Kenya). The Gangwi of Liberia narrate mythical stories of women who are so skilled in witchcraft they leave havoc, war, and destruction in their wake. Since in these myths men come into the world prior to women, the priority is always (conveniently?) interpreted as superiority. Myths about skill in magic are meant to raise suspicion in dealing with women. As a whole, these myths show every sign of having been created by men.

Because of the close connection ethnophilosophy makes between traditional African philosophy and religion, and because missionary religions have had more impact on Africa than has philosophy, African feminist theologians have been more vocal than feminist philosophers. One of those voices is that of Ghanaian Mercy Oduyoye. Writing about African male theologians whose conservative outlook does not allow them to address issues of liberation from gender oppression, she says:

> At times they have even said it is not an issue in their world, where men and women *know their place* and *play their role* ungrudgingly and no one feels suffocated by society's definition of femininity and masculinity. Issues of sexism are supposed to belong to a minority of disgruntled, leisure-saturated, middle-class women of the capitalist West.[20]

Ethnophilosophy, insofar as it is sustained by the traditional African cultural context, supports a framework in which sexism is firmly entrenched and thus offers no avenues to question and surmount the oppressive gender relations. Oduyoye's critical view is echoed by liberationist theologian Rose Zoe-Obianga of Cameroon[21] and by Dorothy Ramodibe of South Africa.[22] By taking gender issues as their point of departure, these liberationist theologians have shown systematic contradictions in the views of male–female relationships in patriarchal settings. One would think these contradictions would be absent in matriarchal societies. Oduyoye's research, like that of other feminists, shows that even among such mother-centered societies as the Akan of Ghana, women's stories are still told from the point of view of men, and in numerous ways males are still implicitly regarded as superior to or more human than females. In the hierarchy of forces, if Tempels and Ogotemmeli are to be believed, masculinity is closer to divinity.

African feminist philosophers would totally agree with the assessments of their counterparts in theology. Unfortunately, the literature in African philosophy at present may lead to the conclusion that there are no feminists. The keen observer would be hard-pressed to name more than one or two philosophers engaged with the African problematic whose focus could be considered feminist. That signals major problems for the contemporary practice of African philosophy. Indeed, this situation becomes an indirect criticism of ethnophilosophy. Insofar as traditional belief systems enable, sustain, and perpetuate the silence of feminist voices, those systems rely on a praxis removed from the reality of the modern world.

In Chapter 5 I propose ways for contemporary African philosophy to mold itself in a manner that recognizes, affirms, and sustains feminist practice.

Aside from feminist critiques, a second class of critics considers ethnophilosophy to be bad scholarship. This point of view is aptly summarized by Dismas A. Masolo's assessment of the arguments made by Cheikh Anta Diop: "The arguments presented by Diop sometimes sound like a joy dance in the shadow of Egyptian grandiosity, an eagerness to prove a point rather than a thorough presentation of facts."[23] And Appiah agrees:

> Yet it seems to me that Diop—whose work is clearly among the best in this tradition—offers little evidence that Egyptian philosophy is more than a systematized but fairly uncritical folk philosophy, makes no argument that the Egyptian problematic is that of the contemporary African. . . .[24]

There is no denying Diop's panoramic gaze and the gusto with which he attacks Eurocentric pretensions. The prejudices under which he labors, however—prejudices about location of *the* cradle of civilization, prejudices about the priority of cultures—do not allow his contribution to rise beyond a systematic counter-European narrative. It is useful for its purposes, but it is not philosophy. If Diop's work exemplifies the best of ethnophilosophy, the rest of ethnophilosophy is to be considered too deeply flawed. What Kagame achieves by his linguistic explorations is at best a deep semantic understanding of the structures of Kinyarwanda. Semantics, however, is not philosophy. Mbiti's "evidence" that Africans have no future time is too sketchy to be generalized to the whole continent. Ogotemmeli exhibits a keen grasp of the culture philosophy of the Dogon community, of teachings known to all the elders, of ritual practiced universally within the community. Such a folk sage is still not quite a philosopher.

Critiques of ethnophilosophy therefore will clearly be seen to be tied to the definitions of philosophy adopted by the critics. In the definitions of philosophy in Chapter 1 we encountered the challenges by the universalists. Kwasi Wiredu's criticisms of ethnophilosophy are echoed by the other universalists. For Wiredu, traditional beliefs (European and African) are a rich source for the development of philosophy. He warns, however, that the source is not the product. That rich source may be utilized in ways that foster either philosophical or mythological thinking.

Ethnophilosophers are engaged in the latter way. Paulin Hountondji characterized ethnophilosophy as a pseudophilosophy for the absence of writing and rational inquiry. More strongly, he objects to the unanimity implied by the methodology employed. The fundamental idea assumed by the methodology in question is the oneness of all people of African descent, a collective consciousness, a feeling of solidarity. This Pan-African solidarity, in its transatlantic versions, reveals itself also in the concepts of "blackness" and "Negro personality" of Edward Wilmot Blyden[25] and also in the writings of W. E. B. Du Bois in which he urges the conservation of the races.[26] The same sentiment of solidarity motivated the Back to Africa movement of Marcus Garvey. Tempels, Kagame, Mbiti, Senghor, Griaule, and Diop all take the cultural and spiritual unity of African people as their starting point. The African cultures they describe are distinctive and are the sum of values shared by the people. The ethnophilosophers, however, do not develop clear definitions of race, blackness, African personality—and hence deal in pseudoconcepts that cannot adequately account for the differences between people of African descent and the multiplicity of their cultures.

Philosophers with a hermeneutical approach add to the foregoing criticisms the insight that a description of blackness, African culture, Negro personality, and so on, cannot be an end in itself. So even if ethnophilosophers were to provide acceptable descriptions and definitions of these concepts, they would still not have accomplished the philosophical task. Serequeberhan, Towa, Fanon, and Okolo regard the focus on a past-oriented reality, the focus on a supposedly glorious past with its traditional symbols and customs, as a diversion from the lingering legacy of colonialism and imperialism. Contemporary Africa is not the Africa of our ancestors. Consequently, traditionalism constitutes an obstacle to a critical praxis whose object is the liberation of Africa. The struggle of liberation must be fought on many fronts. One of those fronts concerns who gets to define the parameters of the struggle. Declaring difference and repudiating Eurocentrism by retreating into traditional outlooks that extol African values and hint at a collective consciousness of an African heritage is seen by these critics of ethnophilosophy as aiding and abetting imperialism. A declaration of difference is not a declaration of independence if it is merely a reaction to, and is confined within, the categories of the West. An authentic praxis will call into question the cultural, political, and socioeconomic structures that have resulted in the dehumanization, oppression, and domination of Africans.

Conclusion

In summary, there is a small core of criticisms made against ethnophilosophy:

1. Reliance on an oral tradition that is incapable of sustaining critical
   reflection;
2. A past-oriented outlook, relying on a fictional glorious past as the
   frame of reference;
3. Uncritical acceptance of tradition, much of which is outmoded in
   the contemporary setting; and
4. Irrelevance to the struggle of liberation:

   ▨ From the feminist standpoint, failing to examine oppressive cul-
     tural practices;
   ▨ Intellectually, failing to rise beyond the parameters of a discourse
     controlled by Europe; and
   ▨ From the hermeneutical standpoint, failing to contribute to cul-
     tural, social, and political liberation.

Of all these aspects, what continues to spark debate is the contention
that myths and proverbs, arts and crafts, somehow reveal the philosophy
of a whole people. The controversial point here is the consideration of
myths, the arts, and music as texts that, when examined closely, reflect
the fundamental structure of people's experience. Myths and rituals can
hence be regarded as mirrors of the corresponding systems of thought.
From them can be learned the social order, links between the living and
the dead, and the community's place in the cosmic universe. If we take
the foregoing as true, the interesting paradox of a philosophy without
philosophers resurfaces. For it is entirely possible for an individual
steeped in the culture and its tradition to remain totally unaware of the
formal structures underlying the web of rituals, myths, and symbols.
Most critics of ethnophilosophy do not deny that philosophical truth
can indeed be gleaned from these cultural symbols and practices. The
difference is that the critics do not admit the individual unaware of the
philosophical truths of his or her culture into the communion of philosophers. For the critics, the proverbs, folk tales, and myths need to be
subjected to critical analysis.

The lesson from all this, and the answer to the question of whether
ethnophilosophy is really philosophy, seems to be that whether philosophy should be written or unwritten, modern or traditional, depends on

the values with which one starts out. Philosophical thought can be measured on one scale by gauging its perceived usefulness. It is dangerous to adopt views whose ultimate implication is a "one use fits all" outlook. A lesson of the ethnophilosophers is that traditional thought may hold important lessons for contemporary societies. Philosophy is culture-relative in so many ways. Care should therefore be taken not to fall prey to anachronistic traditionalisms or to become infatuated with Western definitions of philosophy.

Study Questions

1. Do you think "ethnophilosophy" is a pejorative term?

2. The theses of Alexis Kagame on the foundations of African philosophy, and to some extent Mbiti's theory of the African concept of time, assume a radical position on the theory of ordinary language. Explain what you think the two ethnophilosophers are doing.

3. In what respects is Odera Oruka's philosophic Sagacity different from the "Ogotemmeli paradigm" of an African philosopher?

4. What does Senghor mean by negritude? Was he wrong to advocate this idea?

5. Would you consider Diop's scholarship to be in the best tradition of African philosophy? Why?

6. Which criticisms of ethnophilosophy would you evaluate as the strongest?

7. Can ethnophilosophy be practiced in a way that makes it philosophy in the strictest sense?

Notes

1. Paulin Hountondji, "The Particular and the Universal," *Sapina Newsletter: A Bulletin of the Society for African Philosophy in North America* 2, no. 2–3 (1989): 6.

2. Hountondji, "The Particular and the Universal," 11.

3. Albert Mosley, ed. *African Philosophy: Selected Readings* (Englewood Cliffs, N.J.: Prentice Hall, 1995).

4. Cheikh Anta Diop, *Nations nègres et culture* (Paris: Présence Africaine, 1954).

5. Cheikh Anta Diop, *Precolonial Black Africa: A Comparative Study of the Political and Social Systems of Europe and Black Africa from Antiquity to the Formation of Modern States*, trans. Harold Salemson (Trenton, N.J.: Africa World Press, 1987), xi–xii.

6. Diop, *Precolonial Black Africa*, 1.

7. Diop, *Precolonial Black Africa*, 99–100.

8. Cheikh Anta Diop, *Civilization or Barbarism: An Authentic Anthropology,*

trans. Yaa-Lengi Meema Ngemi, ed. Harold J. Salemson and Marjolijn de Jager (Brooklyn: Lawrence Hill, 1991); and also Diop's *The African Origin of Civilization: Myth or Reality*, trans. Mercer Cook (Westport, Conn.: Lawrence Hill, 1974).

9. John S. Mbiti, *African Religions and Philosophy* (London: Heinemann, 1969), 2.

10. Mbiti, *African Religions and Philosophy*, 17.

11. Mbiti, *African Religions and Philosophy*, 23.

12. Marcel Griaule, *Dieu d'Eau: entretiens avec Ogotemmeli* (Paris: Chene, 1948).

13. Marcel Griaule, *Conversations with Ogotemmeli: An Introduction to Dogon Religious Ideas* (London: Oxford University Press, 1965), 1–2. (Translated from the original French edition *Dieu d'Eau* published in 1948.)

14. Griaule, *Conversations with Ogotemmeli*, 18.

15. Griaule, *Conversations with Ogotemmeli*, 29.

16. Griaule, *Conversations with Ogotemmeli*, 107.

17. D. A. Masolo, *African Philosophy in Search of Identity* (Bloomington: Indiana University Press, 1994), 68–83.

18. J. Goody, "Review of *Conversations with Ogotemmeli* by M. Griaule," *American Anthropologist* 69, no. 2 (1967): 239–41.

19. Griaule, *Conversations with Ogotemmeli*, 39.

20. Mercy Oduyoye, "Reflections from a Third World Woman's Perspective: Women's Experience and Liberation Theologies," in *Irruption of the Third World: Challenge to Theology*, ed. Virginia Fabella and Sergio Torres (Maryknoll, N.Y.: Orbis Books, 1983).

21. Rose Zoe-Obianga, "The Role of Women in Present-Day Africa," in *African Theology En Route*, ed. K. Appiah-Kubi and Sergio Torres (Maryknoll, N.Y.: Orbis Books, 1979).

22. Dorothy Ramodibe, "Women and Men Re-Creating Together the Church in Africa," *Voices from the Third World* 13, no. 2 (December 1990).

23. D. A. Masolo, *African Philosophy in Search of Identity* (Bloomington: Indiana University Press, 1994), 18.

24. Kwame Anthony Appiah, *In My Father's House: Africa in the Philosophy of Culture* (New York: Oxford University Press, 1992), 101.

25. V. Y. Mudimbe, *The Invention of Africa: Gnosis, Philosophy, and the Order of Knowledge* (Bloomington: Indiana University Press, 1988), 98–134.

26. W. E. B. Du Bois, "The Conservation of Races," reprinted in *African Philosophy: Selected Readings*, ed. Albert Mosley (Englewood Cliffs, N.J.: Prentice Hall, 1995), 30–39.

◙

Is African
Philosophy
Unique?

◙

Two questions will be the central concerns of this chapter:

1. Are Africans unique or so different in their experiences from Europeans?
2. Is this difference or uniqueness a positive or a negative thing?

These questions arise because of the obvious differences in experiences
and cultures among peoples of the world and because ethnophilosophers
have usually built their theories around claims of differences. If individuals are guided in their reflection by their cultural experiences, we must
ask if persons who do not share cultures can nevertheless penetrate cultures foreign to them. This is another way of asking if one can enter
alien thought systems utilizing one's own cultural theoretical framework. More importantly, it is to inquire into the grounds on which
evaluations between cultures (superior/inferior, positive/negative, and
so on) can be made. Is it possible to have all the information at your
disposal that makes clear the differences between cultures? If we begin
with the assumption that African philosophy, for example, deals with
questions about the meaning of life and the ways in which people define
themselves (the same questions that trouble other people of the world),
it must be admitted that "African philosophy" is only part of the wider
enterprise of "philosophy." But if African philosophy and intellectual

heritage are seen as unique (from the heritages of other parts of the world), then "outsiders" cannot be expected to successfully penetrate that uniqueness. Any "outsider" who interprets a foreign thought system is going to import into the foreign culture descriptive terms and concepts with which he or she is familiar. Depending on how much these terms and concepts are translatable into other thought systems, the result can range from ignorance to complete misrepresentation. At the heart of questions about uniqueness lies doubt about whether concepts such as truth and knowledge can be communicated across cultures, whether experience is translatable across different modes of knowing. An example of this difficulty is seen every time Europeans encounter African art. Consider, for example, European encounters with African art, as recorded by Janheinz Jahn:

> Gluck for example, praises the "baroquising element of form" in the mask of the Cameroons, the style of which "has understood so consciously how to master the grotesque," while Kiersmeier ascribes to the same masks "little artistic value," but predicates of the works of the Boula a "refined sensibility and technical delicacy" which lifts them far above the works of most African races. Luschan praises the "great grace" of certain Benin heads, while Einstein places them in a "degenerate coastal tradition" which has recovered in the Cameroons in a late primitive rebirth.[1]

The tendency evident in this quotation is a familiar one to readers of catalogs of African art in Western museums, in which African art is judged as "artistic," "refined," "graceful," and "modern" insofar as it is seen to approximate European standards of aesthetics. This is, of course, to miss the subtleties of the styles and aesthetics of African art, the subjects and purposes of that art, and indeed the meaning of art in African social, educational, economic, political, and religious life. In effect, the tendency Jahn notes is tantamount to a failure of Europeans to see beauty and philosophy in Africa. Janheinz Jahn, it must be noted, is among the first Europeans sympathetic to African philosophy. His style is instructive because he recognizes African philosophy in the tradition of Tempels and Kagame, especially in their acceptance of all aspects of African culture as making up a philosophical system. Jahn does not consider African systems of thought unique and therefore unintelligible to a Western audience. To exhibit the seriousness with which he takes African philosophy, he declares, "There is nothing in the African conception of *Ntu* [concept of being] that contradicts the world image created by contemporary science, and nothing that is incompatible with the organization of a society based on the division of labor, technologically sophisticated."[2] Even as Jahn is attempting to make African cultures intelligible to the West, he also makes linkages between African and African American cultures on the basis of some shared "African philosophy." In both cases (that is, the examples of art and *Ntu* used by Jahn), Europeans are involved in an interpretation and evaluation of aesthetics and philosophy. The foregoing quotations are important because they give a glimpse of evaluations whose foundations are never made explicit. Whether the evaluation is positive or negative, all these are examples of Europeans making judgments that express preferences within the framework of their own system of thought. They do not make explicit what they think makes Bantu ontology and a Western ethos either compatible or incompatible.

There are two broader questions that these two quotations raise. If ethnophilosophical claims of uniqueness are to be taken seriously, why should Europeans who do not value non-Western systems care about thought systems incompatible with their own? And what is the procedure for evaluating the truth claims of incompatible systems of thought? These are the issues that the claims of uniqueness raise. The question about why Europeans should care enough to seek and understand thought systems incompatible with their own speaks to a fundamental danger of uniqueness claims. If African cultures and philosophies are utterly unique, as some ethnophilosophers claim, it becomes easy for "outsiders" to adopt an "it's an African thing" attitude as a justification for further marginalizing those cultures and their philosophies ostensibly because of their incomprehensibility. In addition to this danger, ethnophilosophers must address the issue of how to evaluate the competing truth and knowledge claims of these supposedly mutually incomprehensible thought systems.

Uniqueness as Negative: Placide Tempels Revisited

There can be no doubt that Placide Tempels believed that the Bantu philosophy he had discovered among the Bantu of the lower Congo was different from Western philosophy. We saw earlier what Tempels considered to be the outstanding features of Bantu philosophy—it is not explicit, it is not systematic, it does not compare itself critically to other philosophies, and it does not offer proofs in the same way as European philosophies. The chief difference between Bantu and Western philosophy for Tempels is the improbability of finding among the Bantu anybody who offers proofs to support an exposition of the Bantu worldview. This is why it is important that he, Tempels, should be engaged in a systematic comparison of African and Western philosophies. But another feature of Tempels's involvement with the Bantu must be remembered. His ultimate objective in studying Bantu religion, magic, mythology, and ontology is to understand the worldview for the purpose of deciding its compatibility with Christianity. The "danger" of that objective is that Tempels is too eager to find his Christian experience represented in a Bantu worldview. Philosophy is defined by him in such a manner that the conditions for the very possibility of philosophy are European. The first step in Tempels's ethnocentrism begins with pointing out the differences between the systems. Of the European he says, "his reactions are founded upon a complete philosophical system, influenced by Christianity; upon a clear, complete, positive intellectual conception of the universe, of man, of life and death, and of the survival of a spiritual principle called the soul."[3] Whereas the European has a complete philosophical system, African systems of thought do not meet the conditions of adequacy he prescribes. Here is the difference:

> We need not expect the first African who comes along, especially the young ones, to be able to give us a systematic exposition of his ontological system. None the less, this ontology exists, and it penetrates and informs all the thought of these primitives; it dominates and orientates all their behavior.
>
> It is our task to trace out the elements of this thought, to classify them and to systematize them according to the ordered systems and intellectual disciplines of the Western world.[4]

In pursuit of the European task, Tempels extracts from Bantu practices seven principles. From his observations of the Baluba people, he formulates these seven principles about Bantu philosophy:

1. In European systems of thought, "being" or "existence" is the most general concept. In Bantu philosophy, the essence is force—the existence of anything is its being a force.
2. Every force is specific.

3. Different types of beings are characterized by different intensities and types of force.
4. Each force can be strengthened or weakened.
5. Because all forces are radically interdependent internally, they act on each other and influence each other.
6. The universe is a hierarchical order of forces according to their strengths.
7. Beings higher in the hierarchical order can influence all beings of lower rank directly.

If these seven principles do not adequately express Baluba views, Tempels has misrepresented the Baluba, and the question of the "uniqueness" of their views does not arise. However, Tempels points to his long sojourn among the Luba and his careful research into their ways as evidence of his veracity. These seven principles, according to Tempels, undergird a Bantu philosophy essentially different from the philosophy of his experience. There is nothing in his experience to prepare him for a worldview characterized by a hierarchy of values with *Muntu* (the name in Bantu languages for "man") at its highest level, a social collectivism, and an interaction of forces by participation. The originality of Bantu ontology can be assessed based on two kinds of rational evidence—the evidence offered by tribal sages and the internal evidence of the interaction of life forces weakening and strengthening each other. Both kinds of evidence are to be found in Bantu concepts and ideas. Philosophy is present everywhere. In matters of ethics, Bantu philosophy again shows the importance of the interaction of forces. Evil is the diminution of the life force. The seriousness of the evil is determined by whether the decrease in force was intentional, externally stimulated, or unintentional. For harms that occur in the course of day-to-day social interaction, rectification of evil therefore always involves the guilty party's restoring the strength of the injured party. This is because the guilty party, by causing the harm, has diminished the vital force of the injured party. The injured is at liberty to say when he or she feels the life force has been sufficiently restored. Bantu law is therefore strikingly different from Christian or Western law in terms of acceptable notions of fairness. It is not unthinkable that since Bantu life is thoroughly collective, in times of deciding how to rectify a harm, the collectivity determines the compensation. This is very different from European systems in which decisions about repairing harms are made by judges or juries.

Tempels leaves no doubt of his belief that he has provided in *Bantu*

Philosophy something new, something absent in Western philosophy. From the beginning, his attempt to describe the philosophy of part or the whole of Africa is motivated by the desire to seek a synthesis between African philosophy and Christianity. The push for synthesis blinds Tempels to what would be some serious incompatibilities. For example, while he notes that among the Bantu all forces are specific and interdependent, he fails to make the connection that such a radical individuality of forces would be incompatible with Christian notions of the immutability of God. Another area of incompatibility is that among the Bantu, the intensification of the life force of all individuals is not directed toward God but to all life forces. Even when Tempels tries his best to find that all-important synthesis, he succeeds in pointing out differences.

Having established difference, what does Tempels think about it? It is clear from many passages that African and Western philosophy are different but not equal. Consider this passage toward the end of Chapter 1 of *Bantu Philosophy*:

> We do not claim, of course, that the Bantu are capable of formulating a philosophical treatise, complete with an adequate vocabulary. It is our job to proceed to such systematic development. It is we who will be able to tell them, in precise terms, what their inmost concept of being is. They will recognize themselves in our words and will acquiesce, saying, "You understand us: you now know us completely: you 'know' in the way we 'know.' "[5]

We cannot doubt that the meeting of two cultures raised profound questions for Tempels. At some level we cannot doubt his commitment to understanding Bantu culture and to pointing out that the failure of educationists and missionaries to penetrate these cultures was mostly due to European ignorance of their workings. Even those African philosophers who deeply disagree with Tempels cannot fail to appreciate his attempt to contribute to African culture as he understood it. It is in this light that his initiation of the *Jamaa* movement in the Congo shortly before his final return to Belgium in 1962 must be seen. The *Jamaa*, a collection of Catholic baptized couples, was Tempels's final attempt to stress the importance of family as an avenue for breaking down the frontiers between peoples and cultures. Tempels carried his encounter with the Bantu beyond the level of rhetoric into a political involvement. The problem is that despite noble intentions his involvement was not an involvement on equal terms. His best attempts do not prevent him from portraying the Bantu as the junior brothers of Europeans. The Bantu in their primitive simplicity stand in relation to Tempels as Friday stood in relation to Robinson Crusoe. In this relationship of dependence, the Bantu cannot formulate their innermost concepts due to their inadequate vocabulary. The Bantu must wait to recognize themselves in the words of Europeans. Without intending to, Tempels succeeds in reinforcing negative stereotypes about Africa by Europe because of the framework within which he works. One detects an uncharitable comparison between unstated European norms and the obviously deficient Bantu system—all this because the comparison is taking place within parameters not constructed by the Bantu and in terms whose meanings the Bantu do not determine or control.

To answer the questions with which this section began, Tempels addresses his book to "colonials of *goodwill*" to help them cure the impotence of their previous attempts to civilize the Bantu. The uniqueness of Bantu/African philosophy proves also to be its undoing. A colonial of goodwill is still a colonial. Since African philosophy, according to Tempels, is unique, it takes a long time for an outsider to penetrate it; once it has been penetrated, it becomes clear to the outsider that the philosophy cannot be articulated in its own vocabulary. The colonial of goodwill is better placed to articulate it in his or her own more civilized and developed vocabulary. The tragedy in all this is that the European is not entering the world of African philosophy for altruistic reasons or because of any sense of its inherent worth. The lure of uniqueness is merely an enticement to open up a strange world to the colonial mission. If one follows Tempels, the claim to uniqueness of African philosophy proves to be its undoing.

Uniqueness as Positive: Leopold Sédar Senghor

As the earlier discussion of Senghor noted, one of his central beliefs is that the basic philosophy of a culture can explain the various specific manifestations of that culture. Senghor's poetry and other writings have had a profound influence (negative or positive, depending on your point of view) on the self-awareness of Africans and on the perception of Africans by Europeans. Senghor's is a legacy of celebrating the uniqueness of the Negro African. Unlike the European, the Negro does not differentiate between philosophy and culture. For Senghor this is a false dichotomy that the Western tradition falls into because of its fondness for dividing up human experience into compartments. Senghor's distinctive mark on African thought is his theory of negritude. A major part of that theory is his insistence that the people's institutions reflect their philosophy. The organization of family, clan, and nation; their social rituals; and their religious practices are windows to a people's philosophy. Taken together, these things are the sum of a people's worldview.

Senghor well knows that his view of culture and philosophy is despised by Europe. Surprisingly, he does not try to assimilate to the thought of Europe, which does not recognize his negritude consciousness as an equally valuable way of comprehending the world. The negritude to which Senghor retreats emphasizes the importance of valuing one's racial roots. In the context of black/white and Africa/Europe, negritude denies that Europe has a monopoly on scholarship and civilization. The Negro also has a unique contribution to make in these areas. While European thought is characterized by its rationality (that is, a heavy emphasis on logic, reason, and science), Negro life emphasizes emotion. Negritude does not only claim soul and emotion for the Negro. The movement of which Senghor was a main part went further to claim that soul and emotion were the principal characteristics of Negro African people. The contributions of Negro Africans should therefore, on par with the contributions of Europeans, be exposed for the world to see. Emotion and intuition are *also* methods of knowing.

Negritude treats both rationality and emotion as equal ways of knowing, both of them positive qualities. Whereas the European can celebrate logic and science, the Negro can celebrate form, movement, and instinctive rhythms. The Western world has long claimed a monopoly on logic, science, and rationality. Negritude concedes the claim without argument. The only counterclaims of negritude are that the Western world understand as equally positive Negro rhythms in song and dance, and spontaneous emotion. Here is how a contemporary African writer, Michael Echeruo, has understood Senghor's project:

> For the point of Senghor's extended commentary on the movements of thought between France and Germany, between Greece and Alexandria, between rationalism and romanticism—all that effort was a part of a larger commitment: to explain the history of White civilization and at the same time to find a place—and a good place, too—for the civilization of the Black peoples.[6]

Echeruo has noted a feature central to Senghor's work—an accommodationist tendency by which he intends to counteract the preoccupation of Europe with difference. In this accommodation, every culture has its positive qualities—its irreplaceable truths. Rationality is not the standard from which emotion deviates. Each culture, in its distinct and unique way, contributes to the meaningfulness of human life. The African contributions in music, painting, folk tales, wood carving, and dance are equal in worth to European logic and science. Senghor's negritude and its emphasis on a black cultural distinctiveness raises anew the questions posed at the beginning of this chapter. Before attempting to answer those questions, it is useful to revisit Senghor's definition of negritude:

> Negritude is the whole complex of civilized values—cultural, economic, social and political—which characterize the black peoples, or more precisely, the Negro-African world. All these values are essentially informed by intuitive reason. Because this sentient reason, the reason which comes to grips, expresses itself emotionally, through that self-surrender, that coalescence of subject and object; through myths, by which I mean the archetypal images of the collective Soul, above all through primordial rhythms, synchronized with those of the Cosmos. . . .[7]

The subtlety of thought that characterizes Senghor's work is evident in this definition. A careless reading of Senghor's meaning here may lead to the conclusion that he is disavowing the use of reason among black folk. A more accurate interpretation, I think, would have to be that what characterizes negritude is a different kind of reason—a reason of participation. Participation is knowledge of cultural, economic, and religious values by intuition. Two important questions are posed anew by this celebration of uniqueness. Why should anybody who does not share in a particular culture's distinctiveness care about that culture (since, presumably, the difficulties of penetrating that distinctiveness border on impossibility)? Is there ever hope of comprehending a culture that one does not belong to? If the sense of communion and the gifts of emotion rightly belong to the Negro African, a logical conclusion is that Europeans, who are strangers to these gifts, cannot truly comprehend or possess them. To understand the Negro African philosophy of life (negritude), one needs certain principles of interpretation that are acquired only by being steeped in the worldview of a particular black or African culture. If we interpret Senghor charitably, he can be understood to allow for the possibility that "outsiders" may come to full knowledge of a culture

distinct from their own. The only requirement is a sensitivity to the
peculiar characteristics of that culture. Carried to its extreme conclusion,
though, negritude would demand that a substantially meaningful knowledge of culture requires full participation in that culture. Human existence, nature, and the supernatural world cannot be understood in
isolation, apart from the cycle of living and celebration. So too do cultural artifacts such as sculptures and masks fail to make sense outside the
context of cultural life. Ugandan poet and cultural critic Okot p'Bitek
was moved to write the following, at the thought of Buganda royal
funeral drums "away from home" in a museum at Oxford:

> The funeral drums and the rattlegourds grow tired for lack of
> proper [care]—(for which curator can by heating, tune the
> drum for a dance?). The spirits of these drums must die be-
> cause of the everlasting silence. "Don't Touch!", screams the
> NOTICE! But drums are for drumming not mere gazing at,
> for dancing; for celebrating life in festivals. A saint drum, an
> unplayed flute. . . . What are they for?[8]

Okot p'Bitek does not deny that these cultural items can be enjoyed
by the foreigner and in isolation from their cultural context. That enjoy-
ment, however, must be of a very different order in terms of both its
meaning and its significance. As part of a culture, each component contributes to the meaningfulness of the worldview of the participants. But
uprooted from that culture, it takes much more effort to appreciate its
significance. The further removed a person is from the culture, the more
difficult it is, in p'Bitek's terminology, to take "proper care." At this
extreme, negritude's view of culture and black personality becomes ex-
clusivist. Only black people can fully understand negritude. The "it's a
black thing" theme of extreme negritude curiously excludes in the same
way Eurocentrism excludes. Eurocentrism is the view that Europe alone
accounts for the origins of cultivated society and is the seat of wisdom,
science, and reason. On this view, although other parts of the world may
be cultured and exhibit examples of the arts and sciences, Europe alone
is the epitome of reason and philosophy. Eurocentric views of the world
take as a universal truth the difference of Africa and Europe. The culture
of Europe should be the culture of the world. Rationality, logic, and
science are the creation of Europe. The black African world starts at a
different place. The only hope for redemption is for non-Europeans to
throw themselves at the feet of Europe. Incredibly, Senghor does just

that. Without hesitation, he accepts the European definitions of Africa. He is not, however, seeking redemption by this move. This is Senghor's way of making room for negritude at the table of civilization. Long despised and derided, Negro African culture can now showcase its unique social and cultural contributions. To those who viewed Africa as a Dark Continent and the Negro as a child, Senghor's accommodationism has a different view. To quote Michael Echeruo again:

> It was clearly the point that for Senghor as for many other African thinkers, the suggestion of infancy was not synonymous with the notion of childishness and naivete, but with that of promise and innocence. Africa, as other African thinkers and writers continued to say, was the continent of the future. It was a continent growing into its own future maturity. The image of infancy served also to justify at the global level the case for the decadence of Europe.[9]

Echeruo here captures another feature of Senghor's negritude—negritude takes back all those features on which Eurocentrism placed a negative value. Uniqueness is embraced wholeheartedly, only this time it is deemed a positive quality. That embrace becomes the target of universalists, especially Hountondji.

The Dangers of Uniqueness: Paulin Hountondji

If Senghor is the standard-bearer of the apostles of uniqueness, Paulin Hountondji is the standard-bearer among African philosophers who see dangers in Senghor's strategy, indeed dangers in the many variants of ethnophilosophy. There are, of course, other universalists who have been equally critical of ethnophilosophical strategies. Kwasi Wiredu may correctly be construed as warning that uncritical thought systems such as those embraced by ethnophilosophers invariably lead to the three afflictions of anachronism, authoritarianism, and supernaturalism.[10] Hountondji is, however, the philosopher who has most directly and consistently challenged ethnophilosophical paradigms. It is therefore fitting to revisit his work and through it to reexamine universalist assessments of the dangers of uniqueness.

Hountondji begins with a fundamentally universal view of philosophy. He writes:

> I start from the assumption that values are no one's property, that no intrinsic necessity lies behind their distribution across

various civilizations or their changing relative importance; for instance, if science is today more spectacularly developed in Europe than in Africa, this is due not to the specific and unique qualities of the white race but to a particularly favorable set of circumstances. . . . but this purely historical accident cannot justify any claim to ownership. . . .[11]

An immediate advantage of Hountondji's starting point is that it avoids assuming the black cultural distinctiveness that negritude does. Negritude, by emphasizing uniqueness as a positive value, relies on assuming the black world is a unit—that blackness is a real category in the world. Despite the obvious differences among black people, negritude consciousness presents itself as empirically real. Africa and Africa in the diaspora are unified culturally, socially, and politically. The burden is on Senghor and other apostles of uniqueness to prove the basis of the assumed unification in the face of patent diversity. Hountondji is spared this burden since he does not posit an African civilization standing in opposition to a European civilization. We will recall that in defining African philosophy Hountondji's view was that there is no "African philosophy," just Africans engaged in the philosophical enterprise. The cross Hountondji must bear is quite a different one. Consider his burden in light of this passage:

We can re-learn to think of the successes and failures, the dramas and struggles of other cultures, as being our own dramas and struggles. In a word, through the history of our cultures, through their present greatness and misery and through our own sufferings, we can rediscover the adventure of a single and same humanity which has forever been seeking itself and which today more than ever must re-learn solidarity.[12]

The burden of the contemporary intellectual is to stress the solidarity of the African with the rest of the world. Curiously, Hountondji soon falls back into the European system he tries so hard to get away from. The "single and same humanity" Hountondji discovers is eerily European. Recall from Chapter 1 some of his central concerns: there is a difference between oral and literate cultures in the extent to which philosophical inquiry can be fostered; philosophy is an individual activity as opposed to an unconsciously collective one; and science is the highest form of knowledge. Hountondji either does not acknowledge or is oblivious that the values he embraces are prescribed within the parameters of a European discourse. Hastily universalizing these values is an unwise strategy. It is a move that is in many ways methodologically similar to Senghor's celebration of uniqueness. Senghor developed the idea of a negritude consciousness in response to an uncompromising European ethnocentrism that denied to black people and their cultures positive attributes such as beauty and intelligence. The characteristic way in which Senghor and others respond is by redefining as positive the features that European ethnocentrism attributed to Negro Africans (such as knowing by intuition, participation, and emotion). The weakness of this response is that it does not engage or deny the historical realities responsible for the Eurocentric framework. Attributes that have been defined as negative within that framework cannot simply be redefined by Senghor and others as positive within the same structure of cultural valuation. Hountondji too fails to do that preliminary work of questioning the Eurocentric structures as he appropriates European notions of philosophy. Before Hountondji can claim science, writing, and philosophy as the universals to which Africans should aspire, he has a duty to examine the framework within which they were previously developed in a manner that excluded the non-Western world. Hountondji boldly lays claim to an equal right to literacy, science, and philosophy—but fails to acknowledge the implications of the European cultural context of their development. He fails, therefore, to examine Europe's former usurpation of the right of ownership over these concepts.

This weakness aside, Hountondji succeeds in his critique of ethnophilosophy and its celebration of uniqueness. In an essay entitled "The Pitfalls of Being Different,"[13] Hountondji swiftly underscores the dangers of adopting a position like Senghor's. By extension, Hountondji can be seen in this essay as reviewing the main arguments against ethnophilosophy. By way of summary, the dangers of uniqueness according to Hountondji are the following:

1. It is dangerous for one group to wait for another to validate its humanity. By adopting European paradigms as Senghor has done, the Negro African has a humanity dependent on the European acceptance of uniqueness. Acceptance of that uniqueness by others becomes the condition of respect and dignity. Such a conditional respect and dignity makes a mockery of the idea of the inherent worth of all persons.

2. Claims of uniqueness do not question the legitimacy of the colonial situation in which they arise. They therefore become claims for recognition within the same oppressive situation.
3. The literature in this genre is too oriented toward a non-African audience, trying to convince that audience that Africans too have a philosophy, and dignity that is inherent in humanity.
4. Those claiming uniqueness act in a manner that is dangerously backward-looking, as if the most urgent task were to exhume, reconstitute, and defend a static past.
5. Kagame and Mbiti, who start with the belief that every language is also a complete system of thought, verge dangerously on an absolute linguistic relativism. If every language were a different system of thought, every system of thought would be as good as any other. The problem with this linguistic relativism would be with explaining the inferences to be drawn from languages that do not exhibit similar structures. The danger here is the conclusion that different languages present different truths.
6. Traditional African thought is presented as promoting a kind of group mind, a unanimity in social and political life.

The works of Hountondji and Senghor represent opposite positions on the uniqueness continuum. At one extreme Senghor celebrates uniqueness in a manner that is problematic for the way in which difference between Europe and Africa, black and white, is embraced. At the other extreme, Hountondji espouses a universality that is equally problematic because of its uncritical bowing at the feet of Europe. One of the best examples of how contemporary African philosophers can avoid the pitfalls of both ethnophilosophy and universalism is provided by the work of Kwame Anthony Appiah.

Africa in the House of Philosophy: Kwame Anthony Appiah

With his 1992 book *In My Father's House: Africa in the Philosophy of Culture*,[14] Kwame Anthony Appiah (1954–) established himself as part of a growing trend in contemporary African scholarship. The new African Appiah represents has a familiarity with African cultures and can appropriate and defend those aspects of his or her customs that are worthy of intellectual consideration while discarding those elements that have become outdated. This in itself calls for a keen sense that allows one to distinguish those parts of culture that are not "backward," oppressive, or simply mythologies invented for outmoded purposes. The new African is also, by dint of historical accident, steeped in the literature and history of ideas in the West. This is the lot of the majority of educated contemporary Africans. Appiah is elevated above the common lot because his membership in and understanding of both the African and Western worlds enables him to craft a theory of an Africanity that is not bounded by the all too common national, racial stereotypes of what constitutes "a real African." The cover of *In My Father's House* is adorned with the picture of a piece of African art, which the reader discovers in Chapter 7 was exhibited in 1987 at the Center for African Art in New York. The museum called it *Yoruba Man with a Bicycle*. This figure, it turns out, aptly captures Appiah's insights into the place of Africa in world culture. In *Yoruba Man with a Bicycle* Appiah recognizes a

> polyglot, speaking Yoruba and English, probably some Hausa and a little French for his trips to Cotonou or Cameroon, someone whose "clothes do not fit him too well". . . . It matters little who it was made *for*; what we should learn from is the imagination that produced it. The *Man with a Bicycle* is produced by someone who does not care that the bicycle is the white man's invention—it is not there to be Other to the Yoruba Self; it is there because someone cared for its solidity; it is there because it will take us further than our feet will take us; it is there because machines are now as African as novelists. . . .[15]

This piece of art, and Appiah's interpretation of it, symbolizes the complexity of the situation of the contemporary African. An easy conclusion would be that the piece was a commodity intended for Western consumption. Such a reading, however, sells the art short, for it obscures the complexity of the piece. The principal role of African art is reduced by that interpretation to the satisfaction of non-African desires. Analogously, such an interpretation reduces the contemporary African to what Appiah calls Otherness-machines. Appiah's interpretation here closely follows Mudimbe, who has noted that one of the features of colonialism was the categorization of African things "according to the grid of Western thought and imagination, in which alterity is a negative category of the Same."[16] "Otherness-machine" would be a fitting description of the African who sees the most urgent task of the moment as articulating for the Western audience, in a language familiar to that audience, the traditions, social relationships, and other facets of African cultural life. In the retelling of a sentimental glorious past, an exotic other is created and recreated for the West. The reader will recognize ethnophilosophy in a number of diverse but representative works: Janheinz Jahn's *Muntu: African Cultures and the Western World*; Alexis Kagame's work on Kinyarwanda; the wisdom of the Dogon sage Ogotemmeli; and Mbiti's concept of time. By claiming a shared body of beliefs and concepts by the Dogon, Bantu, or Africans generally, these works perpetuate the otherness of Africa.

On the American scene, the same criticism can be directed, to a lesser degree, at the early Pan-Africanists represented by W. E. B. Du Bois and some latter-day proponents of Afrocentrism such as Molefi Asante and Maulana Karenga. Afrocentric theories about difference would seem to reduce their proponents to the principal role of addressing racial difference and its implications. The use of Du Bois as an example here is bound to be controversial because of his subtlety as a thinker. In his 1897 essay "The Conservation of Races," Du Bois develops a theory that recognizes "eight distinctly differentiated races." The conception of race that Du Bois proposes has at its core an assumption that races share a common history. He leaves the lingering impression that races share a lot more than a common history. Problematic though it is, his definition would work best if we read into it the common ancestry of races that Du Bois is not brave enough to openly admit. For Du Bois, each race has a specific message to deliver to humanity. The Negro race must not withhold its special message from humanity, or be prevented from complementing the messages of the white race and other races. Here is a grand vision of reconciling all the races of the world in a universal dialogue, each race bringing to the dialogue the achievements of its history and traditions and contributing its irreplaceable truth. It will be recalled that Senghor too has such a vision.

For Appiah, this talk of races is dangerous because it throws one right into the jaws of the beast. Africans or African Americans who rely on a biologically or culturally based conception of race place themselves exactly where the purveyors of virulent stereotypes have always wanted to place them. Appiah has written extensively on issues of race, and it is therefore impossible to reproduce the subtlety of his argument here.[17] I understand the gist of his argument to be that race—stripped of the elements of common history, common ancestry, biology, and culture, which are often presented as constituting it—reveals itself to be a concept designed to keep people in their place. A shared history does not constitute race because "sharing a common group history cannot be a *criterion* for being members of the same group, for we would have to be able to identify the group in order to identify *its* history."[18] Language and biology are neither necessary nor sufficient. Where does that leave Du Bois and other race theorists? Appiah does not mince words:

> The truth is that there are no races: There is nothing in the world that can do all we ask race to do for us. As we have seen, even the biologist's notion has only limited uses, and the notion that Du Bois required, and that underlies the more hateful racisms of the modern era, refers to nothing in the world at all. The evil that is done is done by the concept, and by easy—yet impossible—assumptions as to its application.[19]

Appiah's discussion of race is instructive, even if there has not been a consensus on the position he arrives at. Philosopher Albert Mosley has, for example, argued in a paper entitled "Negritude, Nationalism, and Nativism: Racists or Racialists?"[20] that Appiah is mistaken in drawing from his analyses the conclusion that there are no races. Mosley, by way of analogies from the animal kingdom, argues for the usefulness (or at least the validity) of the race concept in some of its cultural, pragmatic, and historical applications. In the same vein as Mosley, Lucius Outlaw too in his "Against the Grain of Modernity: The Politics of Difference and the Conservation of 'Race' " argues that there is much in Du Bois's conception of race that Appiah misses. Outlaw thinks it much more fruitful to reconsider the race theory of Du Bois as "part of a decidedly [political] project that involves prescribing norms for the social construction of reality and identity, for self-appropriation and world-making."[21]

Even though there are disagreements of this kind with Appiah, Appiah's point about the dangers of accepting stereotypical views of oneself remains well taken. Such disagreement is healthy and points to the dialectical aspects of African and African American scholarship attempting to negotiate a place in world culture. There is a lesson to be learned even from the isolationist Afrocentrists, the ethnophilosophers, and the Pan-Africanists. For Appiah the way forward is clear:

> But the more important lesson to be drawn, I think, is from one significant reaction of African philosophers to their recognition of the limitations of ethnophilosophy: which has been to turn to what Odera Oruka, the Kenyan philosopher, has dubbed "national-ideological philosophy": toward, in

other words, the reflective articulation of the great ethical
and political questions raised by the struggle through colonialism and toward post-colonial social and economic development. For African-Americans the great ethical and political
questions are raised by the history of racism; and they involve
more than political philosophy narrowly conceived, since
there are cultural issues centrally raised by the African-American identity.[22]

The lesson here is for a contemporary African and African American
scholarship not produced by Africans and African Americans primarily
for a Western audience. If it is to be taken seriously, that scholarship
must take its impetus from the contemporary social and political situation. This new Africanity is not limited by dangerous stereotypes and
thus can promote "constructing alliances *across* states—and especially in
the Third World—a Pan-African identity, which allows African-Americans, Afro-Caribbeans, and Afro-Latins to ally with continental
Africans. . . ."[23] Only then can we understand why *Yoruba Man with a
Bicycle* honorably belongs in a museum in New York.

Conclusion

One of the questions with which this chapter began was why unsympa-
thetic Europeans would care about thought systems that they deem both
foreign and incomprehensible. On closer examination, it is clear that
something is wrong with this question. The world does not owe Europe
anything. The onus of justifying how worthy a thought system is falls
equally on all the members of different systems of thought. The fact that
Europe is in a position to demand such justifications from "foreign"
thought systems (while not recognizing such a demand made by "foreign" thought systems) is itself a sign of an injustice. Uncritical claims
of uniqueness further the status quo. It is indeed the real or feigned
disconnectedness from the rest of humanity that both conceals and perpetuates the problems of social justice. Problems of social justice in the
contemporary world make it imperative for the African debate about
uniqueness to take a crucial turn. Appiah's insight about constructing
linkages across the conventional boundaries—indeed, for Africans to
mold for themselves a transcultural, transnational, and transracial identity—promises to be the way forward. Enough time has been spent debating the existence of African philosophy. Although useful, that debate
has now run its course. In the last thirty years, attention has also been
focused on how European scholarship developed vested interests in its
relations with Africa, resulting in the privilege of Europe over Africa.

Mudimbe has powerfully discussed both the epistemological and ideological ethnocentricisms that were at the heart of European inventions of Africa.[24] This theme has been explored sufficiently in the writings of African philosophers (Wiredu, Hountondji, and Appiah) and politicians (Kenneth Kaunda, Kwame Nkrumah, and Julius Nyerere). Ethnophilosophy, too, in its different stripes, was a response to Europe. But as life in the contemporary global community becomes increasingly interdependent, new social and political questions are raised that should take precedence over preoccupation with Europe. The new world order, so-called, affects African identity in ways unimaginable only a few years ago. The growing interdependence of countries, the population explosion (especially in the Third World), the information superhighway, environmental degradation, the widening gap between North and South, and threats of war in this post-cold war era—all these are major ethical problems facing Africans and all other members of the global community. A failure to grapple with such problems will surely diminish the relevance of Africa in the global community.

Study Questions

1. What characteristics are usually taken to indicate the uniqueness of African thought systems?

2. To what extent do you think these characteristics are stereotypical, if at all?

3. If Tempels was right that Bantu philosophy was wholly different from European philosophy, how could he, a European missionary, hope to articulate it accurately in his book?

4. Do you think Senghor was right to propose and defend negritude as he did?

5. Is there any difference between belief in negritude and belief in Eurocentrism?

6. Hountondji has criticized Senghor's negritude as dangerous. Reconstruct Hountondji's arguments.

7. Appiah takes the middle path between Hountondji and Senghor. Do you think that this middle path is any less dangerous?

Notes

1. Janheinz Jahn, *Muntu: An Outline of the New African Culture* (New York: Grove Press, 1961), 173.

2. Jahn, *Muntu*, 131.

3. Placide Tempels, *Bantu Philosophy*, trans. Rev. Colin King (Paris: Présence Africaine, 1959), 18.

4. Tempels, *Bantu Philosophy*, 21.

5. Tempels, *Bantu Philosophy*, 36.

6. Michael J. C. Echeruo, "Negritude and History: Senghor's Argument with Frobenius," *Research in African Literatures* 24 (Winter 1993): 1–13. For a critical though generally positive evaluation of Senghor, see the discussion by Parker English in Parker English and Kibujjo M. Kalumba, *African Philosophy: A Classical Approach* (Upper Saddle River, N.J.: Prentice Hall, 1996), 57–65.

7. L. S. Senghor, "Negritude and African Socialism," in *African Affairs*, no. 2, ed. Kenneth Kirkwood (London: Chatto and Windus, 1963), 13.

8. Okot p'Bitek, "On Culture, Man and Freedom," in *Philosophy and Cultures: Proceedings of Second Afro-Asian Philosophy Conference, Nairobi, October/November, 1981*, ed. Henry Odera Oruka and Dismas A. Masolo (Nairobi: Bookwise, 1983), 111.

9. Echeruo, "Negritude and History," 12.

10. Kwasi Wiredu, *Philosophy and an African Culture* (Cambridge: Cambridge University Press, 1980), 1. Although Wiredu's point in this discussion is that these afflictions can be found in all societies, the way in which he defines these afflictions makes it clear that an ethnophilosophical mentality is more likely to cause and perpetuate them.

11. Paulin Hountondji, *African Philosophy: Myth and Reality* (Bloomington: Indiana University Press, 1983), 177.

12. Paulin Hountondji, "The Pitfalls of Being Different," *Diogenes, International Council for Philosophy and Humanistic Studies*, 131 (Fall 1985): 56.

13. Hountondji, "The Pitfalls of Being Different."

14. Kwame Anthony Appiah, *In My Father's House: Africa in the Philosophy of Culture* (New York: Oxford University Press, 1992).

15. Appiah, *In My Father's House*, 157.

16. V. Y. Mudimbe, *The Invention of Africa: Gnosis, Philosophy, and the Order of Knowledge* (Bloomington and Indianapolis: Indiana University Press, 1988), 12.

17. For Appiah's latest discussion on race, see Kwame Anthony Appiah and Amy Gutmann, *Color Conscious: The Political Morality of Race* (Princeton, N.J.: Princeton University Press, 1996).

18. Appiah, *In My Father's House*, 32.

19. Appiah, *In My Father's House*, 45.

20. Albert G. Mosley, ed., *African Philosophy: Selected Readings* (Englewood Cliffs, N.J.: Prentice Hall, 1995), 216–35.

21. Lucius Outlaw, "Against the Grain of Modernity: The Politics of Difference and the Conservation of 'Race,'" *Man and World* 25 (1992): 463.

22. Kwame Anthony Appiah, "African-American Philosophy?" *The Philosophical Forum* 24, no. 1–3 (1992–93): 29–30.

23. Appiah, *In My Father's House*, 180.

24. Mudimbe, *The Invention of Africa*, 20–3.

PART THREE

African
Philosophy
Making
Connections

◙

Chapter Four

What Should the Language(s) of African Philosophy Be?

◙

Just as there is no agreement about how to define African philosophy, there is no agreement about what language or languages philosophy on the African continent should be conducted in. The contemporary debates between Africans are predominantly carried out in English and French, and to a limited extent in Portuguese. African philosophy is being conducted almost completely in languages foreign to the continent.

This is itself a curious situation since there are approximately one thousand African languages. Following a classification system developed by Joseph H. Greenberg,[1] African languages are usually divided into four major language families:

◙ Congo-Kordofanian. This group includes the Niger-Congo and the Kordofan languages and the Sudanic languages of West Africa, extending eastward to the Bantu of Central, East, and parts of Southern Africa. Keeping in mind the discussion about ethnophilosophy in the first two chapters, it is interesting to note that the Baluba, the Akan, and the Dogon belong to this family.

◙ Afro-Asiatic. Spoken in North Africa and around the Horn, it consists of the Berber languages of North Africa, the ancient Egyptian, Semitic, Cushitic, and the Chadic languages. As a point of interest this group brings together Arabs, Egyptians, and Ethiopians, who have long traditions of writing.

◙ Nilo-Saharan. This is the family of languages in the Sudanic belt

such as Songhai and Kanuri, and also the Chari-Nile group together with Nilotic northeastern languages.

▣ Khoisan. Spoken in Southern Africa, this family combines the
Khoikhoi and San languages which are characterized by click
sounds.

Greenberg listed 730 different languages. Although his is one of the
most authoritative studies, among linguists there is still no generally accepted definition of language. What some linguists consider languages
others consider mere dialects. The dispute is essentially about where the
emphasis should be. Whereas for some linguists language is an arbitrary
system of symbols meant for communication, for others language is a
mirror of reality, and so an understanding of the structure of language
would lead to understanding the structure of reality. Each of these views
leads to a different way of determining what constitutes a language.
Whichever view one adopts, there are some two thousand cultural
groups on the continent, most with their own distinct ethnicities, religions, and languages. It is now generally accepted that Greenberg's list
was conservative and that there are more than a thousand completely
different and mutually unintelligible languages in Africa. The four language families cannot be shown to have a single origin, and it is unrea-
sonable to assume that a basic unity exists among African languages. This
lack of linguistic unity has had enormous cultural and political implications. The adage that there is strength in numbers has not proved true
in the case of African languages. Consider the situation in various countries, reported by Jan Knappert:

> More than a thousand completely different languages are spo-
> ken in Africa, where almost every nation is composed of nu-
> merous ethnic groups with distinct cultures and religions,
> speaking mutually unintelligible languages. In Somalia only
> three languages are spoken, in Zimbabwe only nine, but in
> Kenya 39, in Uganda and Ghana 22 each, in Tanzania 46, in
> Ethiopia and Eritrea together 76, and Zaire 326. All these
> are distinct languages; dialects are not counted in this survey.
> Nigeria, Cameroun and the Sudan speak some two hundred
> languages each. Unknown languages are still being described
> by diligent linguists. . . .[2]

These numbers show that there is no single language shared by all
Africans—a fact that seems obvious enough to Africans but always seems

to surprise Westerners. Kiswahili is one of the two most widely spoken languages in Africa; it is spoken in Tanzania, Kenya, Uganda, and in part of Central Africa. Hausa, the other most widely spoken African language, is spoken in West Africa. In Africa, one of the features of colonial oppression was control over the use of indigenous languages. The local languages were seen by the colonials as "divisive" and a hindrance to "civilization" and "modernization." Ostensibly because Africans were incapable of rational, reflective thought and their languages were too underdeveloped for such thought, European languages had to replace African languages. The more immediately visible changes took place in the spheres of education and religion. The most pernicious effect of this imposition of foreign languages was that in this way colonialism justified the need for European conquest and perpetuation of its own hierarchical structure of power. Whatever the national differences in the modes of operation of British, French, Belgian, German, or Portuguese colonialism, the result was the same: in their different ways they used language to buttress a Eurocentrism that excluded Africanity and blackness from rationality, philosophy, and civilization.

In the next section I discuss a view of language that criticizes the European imposition of foreign languages on Africa as being particularly dangerous because the intention of that imposition was to wipe out the collective memory of African peoples.

Language as Collective Memory Bank

Language is the mirror of the culture in which it is used. That mirror will, of course, differ in what it reflects depending on whether the culture in question places emphasis on the written word or the spoken word. Within the words, its sentences, morphemes and phonemes, syntax, and semantics of every language are entombed the cultural riches. Ethnophilosophers have long been fascinated by the relations between language, society, and culture. Ogotemmeli reported that the spoken word is the *Nommo* that covers the nakedness of the speaker. Tempels reports that among the Bantu, by means of the word, the *muntu* (human being) commands the cosmic forces and can strengthen or diminish the vital force of another *muntu*. Kagame and Mbiti made systematic examinations of the style and content of specific languages and proceeded to make inferences from the linguistic data as to the existence of worldviews. And there can be little doubt of the influence the negritude poets had on the self-awareness of the African. Words encapsulate the culture as a whole as well as its history. This view of language as a treasury of culture and philosophy is articulated by Joseph Ki-Zerbo:

> Language is like a bank or museum in which, over the centuries, each ethnic group has deposited all it has built up and accumulated in the way of mental and material tools, memories and resources of the imagination. By means of an in-depth and wide-ranging study of the language (both infra- and supra-linguistic), through religious documents, fable and legal customs, medical and educational prescriptions, instruction in craft and technical skills, it is possible to uncover the entire grid pattern underlying a culture or civilization: how they behave . . . their conceptions of . . . love, the hereafter, human destiny, and so on.[3]

Ki-Zerbo's position is ethnophilosophical, as can be confirmed by his other writings. In these writings he takes as evident that a collectivist outlook is typical of African societies. In his "La Personnalité Negro-Africaine,"[4] he states as an evident truth that one of the basic elements of the African personality is the collectivist spirit. The evidence is, of course, linguistic data. African religious concepts, cosmological views, and anthropological beliefs can be discovered through the medium of language.

Herein lies the difference between ethnophilosophers and philosophers. Ethnophilosophers see each distinct language as a distinctly new way of experiencing the truth (cultural, political, and religious). The conviction is that language cannot be understood except in the context of the total culture, and language reveals the way the culture sees its universe. Language is therefore the reality that philosophy expresses.

How then can an authentic African reality be experienced in a foreign language? Ethnophilosophers and philosophers interpret differently the meaning of the statement "African languages are philosophically rich."

For the two clerics Father Alexis Kagame and John Mbiti, a study of their respective African languages revealed the philosophy of the speakers of those languages. Kagame studied the linguistic structures of Kinyarwanda (the language of the Bantu people of Rwanda) in the belief that this was the way to get an understanding of the philosophical categories of the language. In his two major philosophical works, *La Philosophie bantu-rwandaise de L'être* of 1956 and *La Philosophie bantu comparée* twenty years later, the guiding principle is that the unique philosophy of the Banyarwanda and, more generally, that of the Bantu-speaking peoples of Eastern and Central Africa is embodied in their languages. In these books Kagame deduces from the linguistic structures of Kinyarwanda and other Bantu languages what he calls Bantu philosophy regarding such categories as being and nothingness, immortality, causality, and unity. Kagame's categories, or rather the Bantu categories he "discovered," closely follow those of Aristotle. It may be helpful to give an example of the Aristotelian categories in order to understand Kagame's "discovery." Aristotle utilizes the categories substance, quantity, quality, relation, place, time, position, state, action, and affection. Kagame's explorations into Kinyarwanda convince him of the existence of these same categories in that language. His explanation is that the coincidence of categories derives from the universality of philosophy. Philosophy is no less Bantu than it is Hellenic. Although universal, philosophical concepts precede language. Thus language comes to be molded according to universal concepts distinguished only in their contextual and geographical applications. This is what Kagame means when he says language becomes a store of a people's worldview, their philosophy.

Kenyan theologian Mbiti proceeds in the same fashion as Kagame. One of his most controversial contributions is on the African concept of time. After studying the verb tenses in the Kenyan languages Kikamba and Gikuyu, he finds no words that convey the idea of a distant future. The conclusion to be drawn from this is that Africans, since their languages lack the appropriate vocabulary, do not make abstractions about time, nor do they think of time as being of endless duration in its future dimension. Africans are locked into conceiving of time only in relation to specific events. Mbiti advances a concept of time according to which there is an endless past (*Zamani*), a present (*Sasa*), and a very short future. African time moves backwards in the sense that the *Sasa* is constantly shading into the *Zamani*. Mbiti's contribution is significant since he bases his inferences about the African concept of time on linguistic analysis. From this analysis he builds connections between the African concept of time and other aspects of African religions and philosophy.

It should be noted that Kagame and Mbiti present material from only a very few of the more than one thousand African languages. If distinct languages are distinct ways of experiencing reality, Kagame and Mbiti have not exhausted the possibilities opened up by the cultures of the African continent. From such limited samples it would seem premature

for ethnophilosophers to make general inferences about "Bantu philosophy" or "the African concept of time." As representatives of the camp
within the practice of African philosophy that proceeds from linguistic
analysis, Kagame and Mbiti have been criticized on two main grounds.

The first criticism is what Hountondji has called the myth of unanimity. Hountondji decries projects such as those by Kagame and Mbiti
because they lead to the absurd view that all Kinyarwanda speakers, or
all Bantu people, or all Africans who share a language thereby share the
same philosophy. If language is a collective memory bank, Hountondji's
problem is that this seems to imply that speakers of a language have the
same memory. A further absurdity is that although no one has an individual philosophy or a consciously held belief system, all are at the same
time unwitting philosophers (as evidenced by their knowledge of their
language). This is not a claim usually made for or by any of the other
world philosophies. The simple observation that there are many philosophies that have been expressed by speakers of English, French, German,
or other languages shows that the native speakers of these languages do
not all agree. And that is as it should be. Now, if speakers of English are
not unanimous in their choice of philosophy, why then would anybody
have reason to think that speakers of African languages are unanimous?
One imaginable reason is the wish to conclude from the linguistic analysis that Africans and their languages are esoteric and unique. The problematic implications of such claims to uniqueness were examined in
Chapter 3, especially in the discussion of Senghor's theory of negritude.

A second line of criticism against deducing philosophy from language
as the ethnophilosophers do is that to do so is to confuse the container
with its contents. On this view, a language is neutral in the sense that
anything can be expressed in it—often different and even conflicting
philosophies. Language is a tool malleable enough to reflect each person's experience of reality. In their encounters with the complexity of
reality, speakers of the same language bring diversity and divergence to
the common tongue. Even though broadly speaking, it is true that each
society or community or nation has its *weltanschauung*—its worldview,
characteristics, or intellectual orientations—its members in constructing
explanations of their reality give birth to different philosophies.

It is easy then to see the confusion of Kagame's and Mbiti's linguistic
exercises. Let us revisit our earlier discussion of these two ethnophilosophers in order to emphasize the points of the earlier criticisms. Tempels
claimed to have unearthed Bantu philosophy. Mbiti discovered in a
number of African languages a unique concept of time. We see now that

what is "revealed" to them, what they "discover," after their extended searches of African languages is nothing more than what they put into the search. Kagame, schooled in Aristotelian philosophy, discovers Aristotelian categories in Kinyarwanda. Mbiti, a Christian theologian, discovers among the Africans he studies a concept of time quite different from the biblical but one that properly understood makes it easier for him to proselytize in his native land. Kagame and Mbiti are thus engaged not in the production of African philosophy but in semantic exercises. Those within African philosophy who insist on universality and analytic rigor would therefore hold that if the efforts of Kagame and Mbiti are to be classified as philosophy at all, then what they have produced is their personal philosophy and not Rwandan or Bantu or African philosophy.

The analogy of language as a memory bank is therefore not best understood using the ethnophilosophical paradigm. I take up the analogy again later in the discussion of Ngugi wa Thiong'o, but first it is important to discuss a problem that has a special significance in Africa—the conflict over written language versus oral language.

Written Language and Oral Language

One of the tasks of contemporary African philosophers is to contend with the logocentrism of writing. By logocentrism I wish to invoke the Greek notion of *logos*—the idea of a rational principle, reason, intellect, or thought. Although *logos* can be understood as the faculty of reason, it can also be understood as the object of reason (that is, the facts, images, and knowledge grasped by reason). The logocentrism of Europe is constituted by the belief in the primacy of the written word as the avenue for the faculty of reason. What are the implications of this European prejudice against orality? African philosophers and other intellectuals must be engaged in a critical analysis of the hegemony of written over oral discourse that Africa has inherited from her experiences with Europe. With the exception of Ethiopia, Egypt, and the old trading kingdoms of West Africa, the people of Africa do not have a long tradition of writing. The hieroglyphics of the ancient Egyptians was one of the oldest written traditions on the continent. There has also been a written tradition in Ethiopia that dates back to at least the fourth century B.C.—first in Ge'ez and later in Amharic. In West Africa, the old kingdoms of Mali and Songhai, especially during the reign of Sundiata in the Malian empire of the thirteenth century, encouraged writing (in Arabic) to facilitate trade between them.[5] Apart from these few examples, Africa did not develop written traditions. The reasons for this are not clear. Earlier ethnologists speculated that the geographical conditions were not favorable to the preservation of documents. Other anthropologists (and one may think here of ethnologists like Levy-Bruhl) characterized Africans as primitives who could not abstract but understood only by participation. The speculation here is that African belief in force ontology naturally leads to a preference for active, interactive, and dynamic forms of communication (say, the drum) over the static, impersonal forms (the written word). The dynamic language was then captured in the oral literature in the form of proverbs, myths, riddles, poetry, and folk tales.

The question of central concern posed by the logocentrism of writing boils down to this: Is philosophy inextricably associated with writing? Although oral literature is neither read nor written, can it still be considered literature? In other words, is an oral culture whose population is illiterate still capable of producing texts that, although oral, may be considered truly philosophical literature?

The issue of what constitutes a text is a perennial one in anthropological circles, in hermeneutics, and within the tradition of literary criticism. It is not surprising that Africans whose cultures are oral should now be faced with the same issue of orality and literacy. Over the past thirty years a written literature defining African philosophy has emerged, its texts considered either supplementary or complementary to the oral or, in the view of some, completely supplanting it. Concurrent with the debate about identity there has been a debate about what should count as a text and, indeed, on the intellectual merits of competing notions of text. The debate about texts has remained mostly subterranean, only occasionally bubbling to the surface, and even then only as a side issue. When Hountondji defines African philosophy as those texts written by Africans and described by their authors as philosophical, it is important to realize he is appealing to one notion of text. When Odera Oruka interviewed sages in the Kenyan countryside, he was appealing to another notion of text. When Wiredu appropriates Akan culture for his philosophical explorations, he shows yet another way in which texts may be constructed. When Wiredu's compatriot Kwame Gyekye[6] goes back to the same Akan conceptual scheme as Wiredu, he nevertheless uses the culture very differently and thus exhibits yet another sense in which a text may be construed. In the conversations that Griaule held with Ogotemmeli about Dogon cosmology, there emerges still another conception of text—an oral text authored by a tribal sage. Similarly, the work of Barry Hallen and his colleagues with Yoruba Onisegun reveals another dimension of text. The onisegun, traditional healers considered by Hallen to be knowledgable enough to be the philosophers' colleagues rather than merely informants, must make the philosopher raise questions about the interpretation and evaluation of knowledge across the boundaries imposed by the different textual media.

It is usually falsely assumed that in Western scholarship there is unanimity on the centrality of written discourse as text. This has led to the invalid dichotomies according to which Africa is represented as giving precedence to orality over writing, and Europe to writing over speech. In the defense of either written or oral texts, such a dichotomy highlights only the extreme positions. Hountondji's insistence on writing as a precondition for philosophy is an example of an extremist position. Philosopher Paul Ricoeur, exemplifying a moderate position in the tradition of criticism, extends the meaning of the word "text" in a way that reveals the limitations of Hountondji's view. For Ricoeur, the text is the wide variety of meaningful situations and actions amenable to the interpretive work of critical hermeneutics. He writes:

> from the outset the notion of text incorporated features which freed it partially from the relation to writing as opposed to oral discourse. Text implies texture, that is, complexity of composition. Text also implies work, that is, labor in forming language. Finally, text implies inscription, in a durable monument of language, of an experience to which it bears testimony. By all of these features, the notion of the text prepares itself for an analogical extension to phenomena not specifically limited to writing, nor even to discourse.[7]

Taken broadly, discussions about texts cannot therefore be confined to issues of orality and literacy. In the widest sense texts include art, architecture, and music. Correspondingly, notions of authorship must also change. In this expanded view of text and author, a coherent text can then be subjected to interpretation and reinterpretation—activities that are always tentative because of the difficulty of ascertaining the essence the text expresses. The implications for African philosophy should be obvious. Adopting the broad sense of text dramatically increases the sources of African philosophy. Traditional religions, social rituals, architecture, visual art, and the healing arts become texts that can be interpreted coherently only with reference to each other.[8] In an important sense, texts are constituted by contexts. Rather than taking either oral or literary texts as the model of text par excellence, a more inclusive approach is to recognize and allow for different texts to coexist in dialogue. A

broad notion of text implies the existence of and conflict between varie-
ties of texts. Yet it is a coexistence in which a plurality of texts maintain
their voices in a manner that undermines any text that would proclaim
itself *the* "authoritative" text by fiat. To use Ricoeur's language, the
conflict and disagreement between ethnophilosophers and universalist
African philosophers can be framed thus: the former adopt a notion of
text that stresses the prominence of the "work" of text construction,
while the latter rely more on "texture" and especially on "inscription."

It seems to me that African philosophers who insist that texts must be
written adopt an unnecessarily impoverished notion. I would suggest a
more robust notion that allows the possibility of text authorships in oral
cultures where the writing technology is not part of the production of
text. This is a useful way to reclaim the richness of an oral heritage.
Philosopher Richard Bell, utilizing the enriched notion of text, has offered the African palaver as an example of an oral, narrative, and philosophical situation:

> The village model in Africa is a model of free discourse for
> the purpose of making good judgements and for doing justice
> for individuals and the community. These narrative situations
> force dialogue and give rise to human reflection, and they are
> far from uncritical. Each dialogical situation has earmarks of
> the Socratic enterprise; each is formative of the values charac-
> teristic of that community; each reflects the existential tex-
> ture of human life; each dialectically serves to move a
> community from injustice to justice, from wrong to right,
> from brokenness to wholeness, from ignorance to truth.[9]

Authorship of the text obviously takes on a different form in these oral
narrative situations. Texts are constructed not in the medium of writing
but in memory, and fixed there in parables, myths, art, music, and so on.
This, I believe, is a possible insight into the ethnophilosophical paradox
of a philosophy without philosophers. In the oral situation, philosophical
texts are composed in a social context that emphasizes dialogic encounters and the social construction of meaning. No individual participant
pretends to know the truth, and thus each couches his or her opinions,
beliefs, and suspicions in the rhetoric of proverbs, aphorisms, and myths
of the community. In this activity the individual merges his or her voice
with that of the community. By retreating into the oral culture, the
individual acknowledges being a part of a larger enterprise and also ac-

knowledges being a socially situated participant who is an agent in the construction of knowledge as well as an agent in an interpretive process that is creative. The rhetoric of oral traditions depends on the involvement of the audience, their participation in interpretation and judgment. Multiple interpretations by agents steeped in the oral tradition give the text a life of its own, and the final product is one whose author-ity is difficult to fix. The community of speakers share in, to use Ricoeur's terminology again, the "work." It is absurd in this situation for an individual participant to claim a copyright of oral literature in the manner that the technology of writing makes inescapable in the case of inscribed texts.

This robust notion of text better captures the participatory dialectic of lively speech situations. The written word, even written dialogue, is a mark on a surface and therefore seems cold and impersonal. The best writers have difficulty conveying the speaker's attitude—which is important for assessing the reliability of the information that speaker is providing. The oral utterance, however, is in the world of sounds, which is accessible to all in the community (with the exception of those who may be deaf). Wider accessibility alters the framework within which oral utterances are made and how those utterances can be interpreted. This in turn has an interesting consequence for words and symbols. Abiola Irele, a contemporary African writer, has put it this way:

> An important consequence of orality is the social significance of the literature in the face-to-face situations of traditional societies which provide the context of its realization. We need to take account of specialized workers, "masters of the word." . . . We may apply to this special category of individuals the well-known term *"Griot."* The social role and significance of the *Griot* in traditional society is of the first order. . . .[10]

Richard Bell, developing his idea of the village palaver as a dialogic situation, gives an example of the *Nzonzi* who are *Griots* in the setting of a community palaver. The *Nzonzi* "are usually leaders . . . who are known specialists or who emerge on the spot, as 'masters of the clarification of speech.' " By paying attention to the demeanor of the discussants, noting their every gesture and inflection, and chiding and prodding the interlocutors, these guardians of the word perform a func-

tion that is at the same time aesthetic and dialectical. Bell characterizes
their function thus:

> In a word, *Nzonzi* are like Socratic midwives, guiding the
> palaver to just and wise conclusions. The palaver clearly re-
> flects a philosophical situation—it reflects a real critical con-
> flict on the part of its participants to resolve its common
> dilemmas. In the palaver can be found a rich source for philo-
> sophical reflection in the African context that Hountondji
> both underplays and at times scorns even though he lays
> claim to a form of philosophical reflection of a Socratic na-
> ture. These are more than just "philosophical fragments from
> our oral tradition." They are the self-expressed forms of life
> of Africans.[11]

Written language and oral utterance thus clearly exhibit different evi-
dentiary frameworks within which issues such as those of relevance, fac-
ticity, and truth are negotiated. In this connection, we can illustrate
Bell's point by revisiting Senghor's demarcation between European civilization and black civilization. It will be recalled that for Senghor the
chief difference between European and African is that the former distinguishes the object from himself or herself while the latter feels it. How
does this difference manifest itself when it comes to the spoken or written word? Senghor answers in the following way:

> Speech seems to us the main instrument of thought, emotion
> and action. There is no thought or emotion without a verbal
> image, no free action without first a project in thought. . . .
> For the human being, speech is the living and life-giving
> breath of man at prayer. It possesses a magical virtue, realizing
> the law of participation and by its intrinsic power, creating
> the thing named.[12]

To pick up on the point about creating the thing named, the *Griot*
and *Nzonzi* of oral societies by their activity influence how the evidence
is presented, what counts as evidence (content), and who can present it.
Writing, despite its intrinsic value of preserving ideas for a longer time,
tends to encourage an obsession with factuality and truth. This is not to
say oral cultures do not care about finding out what really happened,
but only to say that this may not always be the central concern. The

Nzonzi make use of the palaver as an occasion for the reintegration of social relationships, an opportunity to smooth things over and restore a sense of communication. The combativeness encouraged by the cold and impersonal written word has no place here. The *Griot* may use the speech situation to present interpretive or ideological positions. In the clarification of these positions, the value systems of the community are reinforced or renegotiated.

A notion of text that does not recognize the importance of these implications of orality is impoverished in other ways. It fails to take account of the different ways in which literacy and orality influence what evidence is to be considered relevant. In the oral setting, the relevance of evidence is strongly tied to practical results. Systematic analyses and past experiences of the community are telescoped into a "folk" logic of survival. Right and wrong are important not as abstract concepts but in the proportion to which they make an empirical difference. If, for example, the nomadic Somali herdsman is "wrong," he will not find the water hole on which the lives of his camels depend. On the larger scale, if the traditions of a culture are wrong, that culture will not survive the sustained onslaught of foreign influences. What counts as evidence or proof in these oral cultures is different from what would count in a literate culture. The Somali herdsman must by the nature of his existence adopt extremely practical standards. It would seem then that a fruitful way to think of what the ethnophilosophers call the wisdom of a traditional culture is the pattern of thought that has survived long periods of criticism and perennial multiple interpretations. Contemporary African philosophers should therefore not hasten to follow Hountondji and those universalist or hermeneutical philosophers who summarily discard traditional African thought because it is not written. A better example to follow is Wiredu, who patiently identifies philosophical thinking using traditions as the source, while at the same time separating useful traditions from the chaff of mythological and anachronistic thinking.[13] Writing technology does not exhaust the whole world of text construction, and it is unnecessarily limiting for African philosophers to chain themselves to conceptions of text that enthrone themselves while repressing or denying conflicting interpretations. In a way this is what happens when African writers and artists work exclusively in French or English as their common languages. The further these European languages are developed in Africa, the longer the birth of a literature in African languages is put on hold. So too is the cultural struggle for liberation in its linguistic dimension postponed.

In Defense of African Languages: Ngugi wa Thiong'o

We return now to the analogy of language as a memory bank. Kenyan writer Ngugi wa Thiong'o (1938–   ) argues that the issues of language in Africa must be understood within the context of European domination, marginalization, and exploitation. The politics of language is deeply intertwined with the cultural imperialism represented by Eurocentric domination of Africans and other Third World peoples in the past four centuries. This was a sociocultural oppression that resulted in the social fragmentation and disintegration of indigenous societies on many levels:

> For colonialism this involved two aspects of the same process: the destruction or the deliberate undervaluing of a people's culture, their art, dances, religions, history, geography, education, orature and literature, and the conscious elevation of the language of the coloniser. The domination of a people's language by the language of the colonising nations was crucial to the domination of the mental universe of the colonised.[14]

The struggle for cultural freedoms is thus the struggle to resist continued domination in any sphere. African languages must be enlisted as part of the discourses and narratives delegitimating colonialism. One way to demonstrate the contention that Africans have always had a philosophical tradition is to revive the local languages in ways that free cultural production and expression. Language is the people's collective voice, and African languages become inescapably contested terrains in the battle to either deny or establish cultural identity.

Ngugi wa Thiong'o begins, understandably enough, from the position that all forms of cultural interdependence must be based on the principle of equality and mutual respect. This can happen only within structures that allow the flourishing of the diversity and richness of the world's cultures, within a framework in which all peoples are equal partners. Hence the need to rearrange the Eurocentric cultural order entrenched by colonialism. Ngugi wa Thiong'o argues that English, French, German, and Portuguese should not be seen as neutral languages. They were used as tools of subordination. During the colonial era, "English language and the literature, philosophy, culture, and values it carried was elevated to the skies. African languages and the literature and philosophy they carried were brutally suppressed."[15]

Language reflects a people's cosmology and their perspectives on reality, conveying the cultural beliefs of its community of speakers. Imposing a language on society is a form of cultural imperialism because language conveys important understandings about the way its speakers live, feel, and think—indeed, how they define themselves. Constantly changing to accommodate new experiences, language is a vessel that the people use to navigate through the realities of their experience, their world, and their place within it. To deny or denigrate a people's language is tantamount to denying their very humanity. In Africa, the European languages played a definite part in the denial of the humanity of the indigenous people. The languages of Europe "were taught as if they were our own languages, as if Africa had no tongues except those brought there by imperialism. . . ."[16] If language is the collective memory bank of a people, the European languages were the languages of power that sought to replace African collective memory banks. Thus the more widely the European languages propagated themselves, the more widely their influence pervaded.

Ngugi wa Thiong'o is accurate in noting that the languages of Europe, complete with all their misrepresentations of Africa, were taught as if they were the only languages worth knowing. They continue to be taught in this way today:

> In these countries, English, French, and Portuguese occupy the center stage. They are the official languages of instruction, of administration, of commerce, trade, justice, and foreign communication. In short, they are the languages of power. . . . for this reason the results of our research into science, technology and of our achievements in the creative arts are stored in these languages.[17]

The majority of Africans do not, of course, speak these foreign languages. Yet failing to master the languages of imperialism meant, and continues to mean for them, relegation to the peripheries of power. The people cannot participate in shaping their ways of life, their social institutions, values, and norms. Languages totally removed from their environment, languages that distort the African historical struggles, languages that stifle the creative impulses—these are the African perceptions of foreign languages. Continued debate in these languages only serves to perpetuate the imbalance of power. A return to the African languages is needed to counteract the Eurocentric cultural philosophy that is located and rooted in the Western metropolis. African languages must be enlisted in the struggle for cultural freedoms, the struggle to regain sight of the centrality of language for self-identity. It is important to cultivate African languages to remedy their colonial suppression, to reconnect once again with the philosophy they carried within them. The task is not made easier by the neocolonial states into which African countries lapsed after "*Uhuru wa bendera*" (flag independence) from Europe:

> During the neocolonial stage of imperialism education and culture play an even more important role as instruments of domination and oppression. European naming systems; European language; European theater; European literature; European content in teaching materials; all these areas, so central to culture, are left intact.[18]

Neocolonialism thus makes it imperative that African philosophy is best done in African languages, just as African literature (oral and written) should be in African languages. Liberation struggles must at the very least involve a dissociation from languages that have long been used as instruments of enslavement, domination, and oppression. It should not, however, be a dissociation that is isolationist in intent but should pause and ask, How did we, as African writers, come to be so feeble toward the claims of our languages on us and so aggressive in our claims on other languages, particularly the languages of our colonization?[19] Returning to the African languages will ensure that the majority of Africans who do not speak European languages are not locked out of meaningful participation in forging their identity.

Putting this need to reclaim African languages into practice, Ngugi wa Thiong'o in 1986 declared, "This book, *Decolonising the Mind*, is my farewell to English as a vehicle for any of my writings. From now on it is Gikuyu and Kiswahili all the way."[20] This was undoubtedly a difficult decision, coming as it did after seventeen years of writing in English. Working in the indigenous languages of Gikuyu and Swahili would serve as an avenue for empowering the formerly excluded and downtrodden by involving them in the production of knowledge and making accessible to them the findings of contemporary debates. Ngugi wa Thiong'o justified his decision thus:

> I believe that my writing in Gikuyu language, a Kenyan language, an African language, is part and parcel of the anti-

imperialist struggles of Kenyan and African peoples. . . . I do
not want to see Kenyan children growing up in that imperial-
ist-imposed tradition of contempt for the tools of communication developed by their communities and their history. I
want them to transcend colonial alienation.[21]

Ngugi's move is not the simplistic conclusion that merely working in
African languages establishes the desired literature, history, or philosophy. It is, however, the necessary first step. Indigenous stories, riddles,
proverbs, and myths should be subjected to rigorous examinations to
ascertain their continued relevance to the African situation. Some parts
of the oral tradition are more conducive than others to furthering the
struggle for a better world. Ngugi rightly insists that our cultures should
not be reclaimed wholesale but should be subjected to the most rigorous
critiques from the point of view of the struggling masses. The quest for
relevance confirms his larger point about neocolonialism—in modern
African countries the center of cultural expression is located at and con-
trolled by a minority that is predominantly male, rich, and elitist. This is
to the detriment of the masses, who do not participate as equal partners—a state of affairs that is often justified using tradition and the "wisdom of our ancestors." All this points to a need to reexamine African
languages. Kiswahili, Igbo, Wolof, Zulu, Amharic, and other African
languages, like languages elsewhere in the world, have been employed
in the service of domination and for the transmission of all manner of
values, world outlooks, assumptions, and prejudices similar to those of
European imperialism. At the local and national level, the cultivation of
African languages should not therefore be in ways that promote or reinforce gender, racial, and religious inequality. On the global level the
cultivation of African languages for purposes of literature and philosophy
should not be at the expense of other languages, otherwise the whole
project degenerates into a reverse imperialism. Indeed, Ngugi proposes
Kiswahili as a language for the world because it has no history of oppression or domination of other cultures:

I have nothing against English, French, Portuguese or any
other language for that matter. They are all valid in as far as
they are languages and in as far as they do not seek to oppress
other nations, nationalities, and languages. But if Kiswahili or
any other African language were to become the language for
the world, this would symbolize the dawn of a new era in

human relations between the nations and peoples of Africa and those of other continents. For these reasons I for one would like to propose Kiswahili as the language for the world.[22]

It would be wrong for any language to exist, as Ngugi puts it, on the blood and sweat of other languages. Claims of superiority, expenditure of time and effort in the suppression of other languages—this is what it means for a language to exist on the blood and sweat of other languages. If African languages were to be cultivated under these conditions, they would be committing the excesses of Europe all over again. Ngugi wa Thiong'o calls for widespread usage of African languages as a way to counterbalance their previous suppression.

On the American scene, what Ngugi says about African languages in relation to European languages may be compared to the situation of "black English." Black English very forcefully compels us to acknowledge the relationship between language and experience and raises anew crucial questions about the politics of language. African Americans, unlike Africans, do not now have indigenous languages. Black English developed in the black community as a crucial element in the formation of culture and identity. The linguist and researcher J. L. Dillard sketches the history of black English as beginning in the manner of all pidgin languages:

> Although many of the slaves may not have had to relinquish their African languages immediately, they all found themselves in a situation in which they had to learn an auxiliary language in a hurry in order to establish communication in the heterogeneous groups into which they were thrown. This mixing of speakers of a large number of languages, with no one language predominant, is the perfect condition for the spread of a pidgin language, which is in a sense the ultimate in auxiliary languages.[23]

Over time black English has become a legitimate and effective medium of communication in the black community. Yet the dominant society does not recognize it. This has meant that African Americans must of necessity be "bilingual"—speaking both black English and the dominant language (standard English).

Like Africans during the era of colonialism, African Americans come to understand the necessity of both languages and the fact that there are unwritten penalties attached to using black English outside the black community. Advancement and acceptance by the dominant society is directly proportional to fluency in "white English." Language has been a major tool that the dominant society has used to deny black Americans opportunity in the corporate and cultural life of America. The power of the dominant segment of society or "mainstream" is immense, and that power in America has been marshaled to deny black English the status of a legitimate language in which it would be perfectly acceptable to be imaginative and creative. White English thus effectively becomes a tool to keep African Americans "in their place." Of course, the argument is not usually couched in these terms. The argument against bilingualism or bidialectalism is usually framed in terms of the advantages of unity and patriotism in an America in which ethnic minorities do not unduly draw attention to their ethnic heritage. The advantages of assimilating into the larger culture are touted. The gains of adopting the "common" language are enumerated. As of 1997, twenty-three states have passed "English only" propositions, ostensibly as an attempt to bind their citizens together linguistically.

Amid this it is forgotten that the cost of unity, patriotism, and assimilating to the common tongue is the denial that black English is an equally legitimate language. James Baldwin aptly captured the sentiments of those who speak black English in an essay written for the *New York Times* in 1979 entitled "If Black English Isn't a Language, Then Tell Me, What Is?" Baldwin argues that "what joins all languages, and all men, is the necessity to confront life, in order, not inconceivably, to outwit death: the price for this is the acceptance, and achievement, of one's temporal identity."[24] Clearly, then, denial of black English is a denial of the cultural identity of its speakers. It is also to deny the importance of the cultural heritage and productivity preserved in the language. That 80 percent of all African Americans speak some form of black English, even those educated predominantly in standard English, is a strong indication that the speakers regard black English as a valid linguistic system. Mainstream American society, by its failure to acknowledge black English, reveals itself to be a society that has never really learned to fully value black people and thus understandably has difficulty valuing anything intimately associated with those people.

Black English is the creation of the black diaspora and is the language of the black community. It was formed in the crucible of slavery with the purpose of keeping alive African linguistic and cultural structures.

The ultimate cost of embracing the language of the larger culture is the loss of this cultural heritage. The capacity of a people "to outwit death" depends in large part on their self-definitions and their ability to actualize such definitions on a large scale. It is impossible to actualize an ethnic heritage that is constantly under pressure to assimilate. The "standard" culture portrays particular groups of ethnic minorities as always being acted upon rather than as actors. The dominant culture has been very successful in these unfair portrayals. Baldwin's indictment of America resonates with Ngugi wa Thiong'o's criticism of European denigration of non-European languages. What America and Europe have done leads Baldwin to conclude:

> And, after all, finally, in a country with standards so untrust-worthy, a country that makes heroes of so many criminal mediocrities, a country unable to face why so many of the non-white are in prison, or on the needle, or standing, fu-tureless, in the streets—it may very well be that both the child, and his elder, have concluded that they have nothing whatever to learn from the people of a country that has man-aged to learn so little.[25]

In Defense of European Languages: Chinua Achebe

The impression should not be created that while Ngugi wa Thiong'o calls for a recultivation of African languages Chinua Achebe (1930–) advocates their abandonment in favor of European languages. Indeed, these two renowned exiled writers continue to share a deep love for their continent, its people, and its languages. Although they come from different parts of the continent (Ngugi wa Thiong'o from Kenya and Achebe from Nigeria), each has suffered the ignominy of exile because of that love. It is important to understand precisely where their differ-ences lie because they represent two orientations for a whole generation of contemporary African writers and philosophers.

As early as 1964, in a paper entitled "The African Writer and the English Language," Achebe declared:

> Is it right that a man should abandon his mother tongue for someone else's? It looks like a dreadful betrayal and produces a guilty feeling. But for me there is no other choice. I have been given the language and I intend to use it."[26]

What does he mean that there is no other choice? Achebe means that for all practical purposes, European languages have become the languages of the world. This is the painful reality contemporary Africans must face. Adopting the tongues of colonizers who leave you no other options is not for Achebe a shameful thing. What is shameful, indeed a betrayal, is to interpret this necessity as a sign of inferiority:

> If I were God I would regard as the very worst our acceptance—for whatever reason—of racial inferiority. It is too late in the day to get worked up about it or to blame others, much as they may deserve such blame and condemnation. What we need to do is to look back and try and find out where we went wrong, where the rain began to beat us.
>
> Here then is an adequate revolution for me to espouse—to help my society regain belief in itself and put away the complexes of the years of denigration and self-abasement.[27]

Achebe's work is aimed at both the foreign agents of imperialism and their indigenous collaborators. His first novel, *Things Fall Apart* (1958), treats the advent of colonialism in Igboland, the region east and north of the Niger delta, and the ensuing entanglement of local rituals and traditions with the West. *No Longer at Ease* (1960) continues the examination of the negative impact of Western concepts on tribal life and also on the consequences of adherence to outmoded traditions. Third in the trilogy is *Arrow of God* (1964), in which Achebe develops the theme about the clash between traditional rituals and the customs from "a land no one knew." Achebe's focus shifts to corrupt African politicians in *A Man of the People* (1966). The theme that runs through all these works is that European control of Africa was illegitimate and among its long-lasting effects is a spiritual and political anarchy. As evidence that the "centre cannot hold," Achebe writes about postcolonial violence, bribery, and inefficiency that has been loosed on the African continent. His dilemma is one that faces all African chroniclers of the times. He is a storyteller who wants to rewrite the history of his people—to reclaim that history from the clutches of the colonizer. As a writer his task is to write the history of his people in a way that weaves their collective memory into a life-affirming narrative. But that reclaimed history needs to be told in a language understandable to the colonizer so that the mistakes of the past are not to be repeated. Faced with this difficult choice, it is an act of courage for Achebe to declare in "The African Writer and the English Language":

> I feel that the English language will be able to carry the weight of my African experience. But it will have to be a new English, still in full communion with its ancestral home but altered to suit new African surroundings.[28]

Chinua Achebe is well aware of the weight the English language has carried thus far. The literature in that language has been populated by good white people wandering off into the jungles of the Dark Continent. In those jungles the good intentions of white people (to bring, in the words of famous explorer David Livingstone, "Christianity, Civilization, and Commerce") are thwarted by savages who pose to the white saviors danger after danger. Eventually, of course, "good" triumphs over "evil." The cumulative effect of such literature is that in it an African presence, which is by definition savage and evil, has no independent validity. Africans count only insofar as they help or hinder Europeans. They are not actors. They are merely the acted upon. Being basically nonpersons, they are not really interested in things normal human beings are interested in—good education, political participation, social and economic well-being. The English language carried this immense weight of colonial narrative that denied the African a sense of autonomy in having and exercising deliberative capacities. These narratives erected for the African a false primitive simplicity that in turn justified European control. This was the start of a vicious circle in which European control justified itself by claiming that Africans had not shown the ability to control themselves—the absurd situation in which colonialism justifies itself as the guardian of democracy. Chinua Achebe is therefore not naive in his decision to use English as the tool for decolonizing African culture. His solution to the language problem is to employ a "new English" featuring African proverbs, traditions, conversations, and songs. In Achebe's hands, Igbo proverbs (Wisdom is like a goatskin bag; every man carried his own;[29] If one finger brings oil, it soils the others;[30] The earthworm is not dancing, it is only its manner of walking;[31] An animal whose name is famous does not always fill a hunter's basket;[32] The goat owned in common dies of hunger[33]) are masterfully transformed in such a way that they are made to express universal ideas and concepts. As Achebe says, proverbs are the palm oil with which words are eaten.

Thus, the English language is used to express traditional wisdom and becomes a bridge between two traditions.

Achebe's decision to use English can, I think, be defended on other grounds. European languages can be considered languages of the world because of historical accidents whose harm has already been done. On the continent of Africa, literature and philosophy are conducted as academic enterprises under circumstances in which the colonial legacy has ensured that the language of instruction, the history, and the content of the disciplines are mostly foreign. The retreat of the European powers to Europe in the late 1950s and early 1960s did not mean they relinquished control over their former colonies. In many practical ways, and most importantly on the question of language, they retain control. Achebe's admission that he has "no choice" is an acknowledgment of this state of affairs. Instead of giving up, however, he chooses to wage the struggle within these constraints. This is not a sign of weakness or of selling out. It is proof of a keen appreciation of one's circumstances.

In addition, increasing numbers of Africans find themselves unable or unwilling to live with the problems facing young African nations— tribalism (or, using the more refined euphemism, geopolitics), corruption at all levels of government, demagoguery, second-class treatment of women, and ballooning levels of foreign debt. A serious engagement with these issues exposes the intellectual to government retaliation, which for Ngugi wa Thiong'o and Chinua Achebe has resulted in exile. To choose exile or to be forced into it is to be immersed in a foreign culture in which one really has "no choice" about the language one uses. African writers and philosophers in this situation still have a commitment to contemporary Africa and its suffering. Yet they must convey that suffering to audiences in the foreign culture in languages foreign to the suffering continent.

Even if one considers those Africans not in exile, there are, for the time being, seemingly insurmountable practical difficulties in producing works of literature or philosophy in African languages. One of these problems is the smallness of the audience. Communities of speakers of the different languages reside mainly within the different countries—and within these countries only in specific regions. An example could be made here of Odera Oruka's interviews with Kenyan sages, published as *Sage Philosophy: Indigenous Thinkers and Modern Debate on African Philosophy.*[34] These sages, even if they knew about each other, could not talk to each other because they had no common language. This mutual unintelligibility makes it uneconomical for academic work to be done in African languages and limits its impact. There are virtually no journals or publications in these languages inside or outside Africa.[35] As a practical matter, then, anybody who works in African languages will be limited to the skimpiest of audiences in terms of both geography and numbers. To reach a wider audience, the African is forced to translate into the European languages or to bypass African languages completely by publishing only in English, French, or German.

It should be clear from the foregoing that Chinua Achebe and other writers who choose to do their work in European languages are not denying the philosophical richness of African languages. What they do effectively is to point out the practical costs of developing these languages if their richness is to be communicated to the global community. There is much to be gained by promoting interaction in African languages—but much more to be lost.

Conclusion

African philosophers have been a little late in proposing their solutions to Africa's vexing language problems. This is not surprising if one understands that philosophers have hardly discussed the problems of language in the serious manner African literary figures like Ngugi wa Thiong'o and Chinua Achebe have. Yet these questions have been raised time and again. The work of Kagame and Mbiti forces us to ask where language ends and philosophy begins, to distinguish semantic exercises from philosophical analyses. The work of writers who use African languages indirectly invite us to discuss the values of oral as opposed to written literature (or indeed where these values intersect) and the cultural underpinnings of the valuation process. There are also issues in language usage that transcend local communities, making connections between Africa and Africa in the diaspora. It is important to take seriously the linkages between James Baldwin's America and Ngugi wa Thiong'o's Africa in terms of the deconstructive hermeneutics in which they both engage.

In short, to take a side in answering the question about which language(s) African philosophy should be done in is to present a voice in the struggle for cultural identity.

Possible directions to take with this question would be to follow Odera Oruka's method of research. Interviewing sages in their vernacular tongues will prevent the tragedy that Africans have captured in the proverb that whenever an old person dies, a whole library burns down. Secondly, there needs to be serious debate about the solutions already presented. An example of such a solution is to be found in Wole Soyinka's *Art, Dialogue, and Outrage*.[36] Presenting solutions is a first step that should be followed by a sustained dialogue about those solutions. It is time philosophers joined the debate represented by Ngugi wa Thiong'o and Chinua Achebe.

Study Questions

1. Mbiti's theory of the African concept of time assumes a radical position on the theory of ordinary language. What does Mbiti present as the African concept of time? What are his assumptions?

2. The written and the oral are different ways of language usage. Does the term "different" necessarily connote linguistic sophistication or superiority of one form over another?

3. What are the differences between oral and written texts?

4. Explain Ngugi wa Thiong'o's idea that language is a people's collective voice.

5. Is black English in America being denied legitimacy in the same way African languages were under colonialism? Are the situations of black English and African languages comparable?

6. If you were to take sides between Ngugi wa Thiong'o's arguments for using African languages and Chinua Achebe's counterarguments for using European languages, which side would you take?

Notes

1. Joseph H. Greenberg, *The Languages of Africa* (Bloomington: Indiana University Press, 1966).

2. Jan Knappert, *African Mythology: An Encyclopedia of Myth and Legend* (London: Diamond Books, 1995), 12.

3. Joseph Ki-Zerbo, ed., *General History of Africa, Vol. 1: Methodology and African Prehistory* (Berkeley: University of California Press/UNESCO, 1981, 1990), 94.

4. Joseph Ki-Zerbo, "La Personnalité Negro-Africaine," *Présence Africaine*, 41 (1962): 137–43.

5. Robert Cancel, "African-Language Literatures: Perspectives on Culture and Identity," in *A History of Twentieth-Century African Literatures*, ed. Oyekan Owomoyela (Lincoln and London: University of Nebraska Press, 1993), 286.

6. Kwame Gyekye, *An Essay on African Philosophical Thought: The Akan Conceptual Scheme*, rev. ed. (Philadelphia: Temple University Press, 1995).

7. Paul Ricoeur, *Hermeneutics and the Social Sciences*, ed. and trans. John B. Thomson (Cambridge: Cambridge University Press, 1981), 37.

8. Parker English and Nancy Steele Hamme, "Using Art History and Philosophy to Compare a Traditional and a Contemporary Form of African Moral Thought," *Journal of Social Philosophy* 27, no. 2 (Fall 1996): 204–33.

9. Richard H. Bell, "Narrative in African Philosophy," *Philosophy* 64 (1989): 373.

10. Abiola Irele, "The African Imagination," *Research in African Literatures* 21 (Spring 1990): 56.

11. Bell, "Narrative in African Philosophy," 374–5.

12. Parker English and Kibujjo M. Kalumba, eds., *African Philosophy: A Classical Approach* (Upper Saddle River, N.J.: Prentice Hall, 1996), 48.

13. Kwasi Wiredu, *Cultural Universals and Particulars: An African Perspective* (Bloomington: Indiana University Press, 1996).

14. Ngugi wa Thiong'o, *Decolonising the Mind: The Politics of Language in African Literature* (Portsmouth, N.H.: Heinemann, 1986), 16.

15. Ngugi wa Thiong'o, *Barrel of a Pen: Resistance to Repression in Neo-Colonial Kenya* (Trenton, N.J.: Africa World Press, 1983), 82.

16. Ngugi wa Thiong'o, *Moving the Centre: The Struggle for Cultural Freedoms* (Portsmouth, N.H.: Heinemann, 1993), 35.

17. Ngugi wa Thiong'o, *Moving the Centre*, 37.

18. Ngugi wa Thiong'o, *Barrel of a Pen*, 96–7.

19. Ngugi wa Thiong'o, *Decolonising the Mind*, 9.

20. Ngugi wa Thiong'o, *Decolonising the Mind*, xiv.

21. Ngugi wa Thiong'o, *Decolonising the Mind*, 28.

22. Ngugi wa Thiong'o, *Moving the Centre*, 41.

23. J. L. Dillard, *Black English: Its History and Usage in the United States* (New York: Random House, 1972), 74.

24. Thomas Klein, Bruce Edwards, and Thomas Wymer, eds., *Great Ideas: Conversations Between Past and Present* (Fort Worth: Holt, Rinehart and Winston, 1991), 652.

25. Klein, Edwards, and Wymer, *Great Ideas*, 653.

26. Chinua Achebe, *Morning Yet on Creation Day* (London: Heinemann, 1975).

27. Achebe, *Morning Yet on Creation Day*, 44.

28. Achebe, *Morning Yet on Creation Day*, 44. This whole collection is an example of the new English he proposes to use. It must be an English that incorporates African proverbs and the experiences those proverbs represent.

29. Chinua Achebe, *Arrow of God* (New York: Anchor Books, 1989), 16.

30. Chinua Achebe, *Things Fall Apart* (New York: Anchor Books, 1994), 125.

31. Chinua Achebe, *Anthills of the Savannah* (New York: Anchor Books, 1987), 145.

32. Achebe, *Anthills of the Savannah*, 111.

33. Achebe, *Anthills of the Savannah*, 33.

34. H. Odera Oruka, ed., *Sage Philosophy: Indigenous Thinkers and Modern Debate on African Philosophy* (Leiden: E. J. Brill, 1990).

35. One notable exception is the Gikuyu journal *Mutiiri* started by Ngugi wa Thiong'o when he stopped writing in English. Despite all the foregoing problems, the journal continues to be in circulation.

36. Wole Soyinka, *Art, Dialogue, and Outrage* (New York: Pantheon, 1994).

◙

Are There Connections Among African, African American, and Feminist Philosophies?

◙

African American theologian William R. Jones argued in "The Legitimacy and Necessity of Black Philosophy: Some Preliminary Considerations"[1] that the experience, history, and culture of black folk in America are ingredients that make possible, indeed necessary, a special approach to philosophizing. This special approach, black philosophy, takes its beginnings from the historical fact that the experience of African Americans as a racial minority has either been devalued in the discipline of philosophy, or omitted from its concepts and institutions. Authentic black philosophy must therefore be antagonistic to mainstream philosophy because the task of affirming black perspectives directly challenges the racism and exclusionary tendencies that have characterized philosophy as a discipline. African philosophy finds itself in an exactly similar situation.

The point has been made in earlier chapters that because of colonial and other imperialist adventures in Africa a political dimension is always at the heart of debates within African scholarship. European occupation forced a choice upon Africans. They could either embrace the difference (from Europeans) attributed to them by colonial discourse, or they could deny any difference and assert the equal worth of their humanity. Arguing for the existence of indigenous African philosophies became in this context more than a scholarly exercise—it became a crucial part of the process of reclaiming African humanity. Philosophy became both the search for and the articulation of an identity. The whole enterprise does not arise in a vacuum. Colonialism was, and neocolonialism continues to be, an assault on the consciousness of the African. Any attempt to understand the defensive tone of some of the writings in African philosophy must take into account colonial characterizations of Africa and Africans as grotesque, primitive, and lacking in rationality, philosophy, or any other redeeming qualities. These systematic misrepresentations were themselves part of a thoroughgoing linguistic and cultural imperialism. It follows, then, that what is at stake in this debate transcends dispassionate quibbling on the meaning of philosophy.

Seen as a struggle against colonialism, domination, and marginalization, a strategy that suggests itself is the coming together of Africans, African Americans, and feminists. The same dialectic that Europe forced on Africa was forced on women and African Americans, and this makes for an intersection of the concerns of these groups. Throughout the history of Western ideas Africans, African Americans, blacks in the diaspora, and women have been defined into roles of "otherness." The commonality of their concerns lies in the deconstructive nature of their various attempts to challenge the definitions that have placed them, and work to keep them, in positions of marginality. The concept of deconstruction is here to be understood as the struggle to offer insights into the structures of the recognition or nonrecognition of moral and political worth attached to "otherness." It is the attempt to understand that although women and folk of color are historically situated, their oppression has been aided in large part by a model of philosophizing that treats itself as generic and its structures and categories of thought as neutral. Deconstruction is therefore the questioning of how Eurocentric philosophizing shapes and influences meanings and social forms of power.

Deconstruction poses a serious challenge to traditional philosophy because its methods nudge traditional philosophy to understand others without assimilating their otherness and to appreciate a process of interpretation that, while implicated in the hegemonic stance, can nevertheless achieve reflective distance and a critique of power. One of the aims of this deconstruction is the attainment of the right of the previously marginalized to occupy a space in the mainstream. Yet even in contesting the definitions of "others," there is need to maintain a sense of balance. Africans, African Americans, and women face the danger of articulating identities defined principally by the role of otherness. There is indeed firmer ground for linkages between these groups than reliance on a solidarity born of an amorphous notion such as otherness. In their relationships with the Western world, these and other groups have occupied subordinate positions. Denied a voice, legitimacy, and the right to self-representation, each group now labors under the burden of hegemonic constructions of the West. In their different ways African philosophy, African American social and political thought, and feminism provide narratives delegitimating the prior oppressive misrepresentations that claimed universality for themselves. The deconstructive movements are a response to the canonical texts and practices that marginalized non-Europeans and women while claiming to be speaking for all humanity. Linkages between the formerly marginalized would prove invaluable because of the potential they hold for cooperation. In this respect of learning from those who have shared similar experiences, the contemporary African has the advantage of being able to access the experiences of African American intellectuals like W. E. B. Du Bois, E. Franklin Frazier, John Hope Franklin, Frederick Douglass, Booker T. Washington, Marcus Garvey, Richard Wright, James Baldwin, and those much closer to our time like Ralph Ellison, Albert Murray, Martin Luther King, Jr., Malcolm X, Cornel West, and Henry Louis Gates. In the same spirit of learning from and connecting with feminism within the African American experience, the contemporary African has the benefit of the intellectual work of the nineteenth-century women Fannie Barrier Williams, Ida B. Wells-Barnett, Fannie Jackson Coppin, Anna Julia Cooper, and those much closer to our time like Alice Walker, Maya Angelou, Audre Lorde, Toni Morrison, Angela Davis, Patricia Williams, and bell hooks. There is much to learn also from the work of other contemporary feminist writers like Sandra Harding, Nancy Chodorow, Seyla Benhabib, Alison Jaggar, Elizabeth Spelman, and Carol Gould.

Although there are differences in the specifics, there is a convergence of interests in the deconstructive aspects of African, African American, and feminist philosophies because they are all engaged in uncovering hidden metaphysical and politicophilosophical presuppositions. They are natural allies, though not often in practice, in their quest to dismantle the problematic hierarchies and binary oppositions of the dominant narratives. They are on the same side since they are each in a sense "outside" voices with insights that they hope will radically transform the exclusionary mainstream canonical texts and narratives. Though these enterprises pursue similar goals, there has been surprisingly little concerted effort to see their patterns as linked. By accident or design, debates within the different enterprises go on disconnected from one another. The African experience with "divide and rule" colonial strategies should be a warning to the dangers of a forced or chosen isolationism that sees similarly oriented enterprises as disconnected and disparate. It should be clear from the past that the political dimensions of these enterprises come sharply into focus when they are juxtaposed as different parts of the same struggle. Clarity is gained in two ways. First, by making connections with movements that share the same underpinnings, participants in the different movements gain a deeper understanding of their own movement. More importantly, however, trying to make these linkages inevitably reveals the ways in which hegemonic forms of authority, knowledge, and institutional and discursive practices have thus far been operative. Such linkages show that marginalization does not happen at random. What becomes clear are the underlying structures (cloaked in the garb of objectivity and neutrality), in thought or action, operative in the narratives that are used as tools for rallying, uplifting, and glorifying one group while alienating, subordinating, and denigrating all others.

Connections with African American Philosophy: A Tradition Born Out of Struggle

> Philosophic texts, if products of social groups doggedly fighting to survive, are texts born of struggle. They must cut through the jungle of oppressive deeds to the accompanying labyrinth of words masking the nature of deeds. Fraught with controversial intuitions that reflect the coming accepted beliefs of the new world, such texts challenge prevailing ways of viewing the world.[2]

I begin this section with the words the African American philosopher Leonard Harris used to introduce his anthology, which has become a landmark in African American scholarship. What Harris has amply succeeded in making evident is that within the African American experience professional philosophers have not had the monopoly on raising the philosophical questions surrounding black existence in America. There were, of course, the academically trained like W. E. B. Du Bois (1868–1963) in sociology and Alain L. Locke (1886–1954) in philosophy. But there were also the nonacademic (who can be considered philosophical only in the broadest sense of the term) like Frederick

Douglass (1817–1895), and Booker T. Washington (1856–1915). The common denominator in African American intellectual activity has been a search for the meaning of existence in the Americas and a concern with social transformation. The race problem, the question of black suffrage, assimilation, accommodation—these are the pressing philosophical problems recurrent in African American life. Explaining and interpreting these problems, African Americans have forged on with the struggle for self-definition. Whether by professional or lay philosophers, that struggle has always been against the twin influences of class and racial oppression. Leonard Harris accurately summarizes what philosophy in the contest of oppression has been and continues to be:

> Philosophy is invariably tied to social reality. It is not uncommon for it to be formed by social dissatisfaction and the demise of stable institutions. Nor is it uncommon for it to address the critical issues facing the parent society. . . . It is possible that some arguments are more than cute tricks with language reflecting social quirks or propaganda disguises for social movements. If so, methods of justification might merit emulation, and conclusions, warrant believing and directing actions. The history of Afro-American philosophy should be understood both as a mirror of changing social realities and a matrix of irreducible arguments attuned to the need for human liberation.[3]

African American experience shows incredible similarity to African colonial experience. Those who have undergone either of these experiences share the feature of being defined by the dominant society as ontologically different (that is, inferior). This attack on African American consciousness continues in contemporary social and cultural institutions. In his more recent work Harris warns of the dearth and near-invisibility of black philosophers in academic American philosophy. Indicative of the continuing struggle was the flurry of responses, some of which were implicitly rude, drawn by his 1995 tongue-in-cheek article " 'Believe It or Not' or The Ku Klux Klan and American Philosophy Exposed."[4] Harris underscores the sad state of contemporary academic American philosophy with these observations:

- "There are no Blacks on the faculty in the Philosophy Department at any of the eight Ivy league universities and no Blacks on the faculty in the Philosophy Department at nine of the eleven Big Ten Universities."[5]

- There are only two black philosophers (Lucius Outlaw and Bernard Boxill) holding either endowed chairs or distinguished professorships vested in philosophy departments.
- No predominantly black university awards a degree in philosophy above the level of the B.A.[6]
- Although there are no rules, laws, or state requirements, exclusion of the works of blacks like Alain L. Locke or David Walker from courses titled "American Philosophy" "just seem[s] to magically happen."[7]

These observations point to an ominous trend within what Harris identifies as a practice of philosophy perilously akin to a conspiracy. To the keen observer, American philosophy would seem to operate, either by chance or by design, in ways that are patriarchal, oppressive, and racist. The practical consequences of that operation are dire:

> American philosophers almost never mentor, graduate, cite, employ, or promote non-whites, no matter how firmly such persons stand on the common ground of American/European cultural, intellectual, and moral traditions. When it is time to grant honors, such as professorships, endowed chairs, American philosophers tend to show deference to individuals that fit the proper racial kind and relegate others to the kitchen.[8]

Practical exclusion of this kind is obviously harmful because it is a *prima facie* sidelining of the excluded group, rendering them powerless because of their disconnection from the dominant cultural and political institutions. In that sense it is more difficult to be engaged in concrete projects of self-definition and liberation. However, there are deeper harms attached to this black invisibility in American philosophy. Exclusion serves as an attack on the consciousness and the intellectual/cultural identity. After Harris's article appeared, a particularly revealing response was not long in coming. It was revealing especially because it seemed to reinforce Harris's claims even as it purported to refute them. The author said, in part:

> Are Whites accountable for the fact that there are so few Blacks in philosophy that hold academic positions? I think

not. Given the fact that barely 1% of the APA membership is Black, what does he expect. Harris further complains that there are no Black graduate students in the top fourteen departments producing the majority of Ph.D.'s. Whose fault is this? Oh yes, I forgot, American Philosophy's. Perhaps philosophy is just not that attractive to Blacks.[9]

The extremely small numbers of blacks in the field of philosophy coupled with the fact that the discipline appears unattractive to the vast majority are precisely the issues of concern to Harris. These statistics about numbers of African Americans in the academy for him point not only to physical and practical disadvantage but also to a denial of humanity. Philosophical reflection here calls for a connection between theory and practice. A little reflection shows that American philosophy has tended to encourage views of itself that are quite at variance with its actual practice. Failing to philosophize in this situation leads to a failure to see the connection between the African American condition and the global historical struggles of liberation. African American liberation struggles can be informed by the struggles of Africans and women who have been similarly dispossessed. Leonard Harris eloquently captures this important point:

> Taken collectively, works by black philosophers are readable as a text on the Afro-American experience; individual articles, symbols telling a tale woven in history's fabric. The tale, at its roots, is of an eclectic process never disposed to free itself from the conceptual shackles that bind oppressed and oppressor. That process of conceptual liberation parallels the concrete movement of the African diaspora in America from chattel to segregated minority, to a minority with a class structure similar to society at large save the burden of racism. As a social phenomenon, the works of Afro-American philosophers are archetypal of social reality and as such form and help shape the reality that has become American philosophy.[10]

Herein lies the similarity of the global liberation movements. The enslavement of Africans, the subordination of women: the philosophical texts of these experiences parallel those of African American philosophy. If Harris is right in these observations, American philosophy has developed as a mirror image of a dominant society that equates white identity with racial superiority. The employment picture, too, resembles the old racial stereotypes according to which white identity connotes hard work, independence, discipline, intelligence, and responsibility. The color line in employment, in addition to its harmful result of economic marginalization, perpetuates disadvantage. Disadvantaged people without either employment or connections to the more advantaged are likely to remain disadvantaged.

Another distinguished African American philosopher, Lucius Outlaw, has taken the observations of Leonard Harris further by applying the method of critical hermeneutics to the examination of how African American philosophy ties in to American philosophy. The hermeneutical method unmasks the implicitly held presuppositions about "philosophy" that make it possible for the writings of African Americans to be routinely excluded from the corpus of American philosophy. Ever aware of the position of marginality to which African American experience has been relegated, Outlaw critically reviews the strategies that have been employed within African American philosophy in relating to the hegemonic canonical texts of European and Euro-American philosophy. He writes:

> The presentation of African-American intellectual legacies and practices as examples of philosophy makes a lie of the denials and disregard of the existence of African-American philosophy and forces a redefinition of "philosophy" through an extension of its denotative range. This contradicts the screeching silence voiced by many of the European-descended gatekeepers to, and executors of, Americans' intellectual heritages.[11]

African American philosophy challenges the definitions of the gatekeepers whose interest is in maintaining the status quo. Again, there are obvious parallels to be drawn between African, African American, and feminist defenses of their legitimacy. The arguments for legitimacy in each case unearth the hidden presuppositions about the nature of philosophy. Yet in all these cases the struggle for legitimacy takes many forms. In contending with the claims of power and authority, blacks and women find themselves challenging the orthodoxies of the dominant frames of reference. European claims of transcendental authority have functioned in two ways: on the minus side the effect has been (sometimes active, but often indirect) repression of alternative expression and the silencing of differing modes of knowledge production; yet on the plus side, that very repression and silencing served to encourage the construction of discourses of opposition that in their proclamations of independence have drawn attention to the limiting character of knowledge constituted according to Eurocentric paradigms and categories. African American struggles for representation have opened up assimilation accommodation, pluralism, and nationalism as coping strategies and as possible (either as contending or complementary) directions for construction of self-image. These are moves that can be and have been appropriated by feminists and Africans. So it is useful to understand their implications.

Lucius Outlaw describes assimilation in this way:

> In its most extreme form, the assimilationist position calls for the eventual disappearance of all factors which make people of African descent identifiable as such. Psychologically this extreme position is based on an equally extreme form of self-hatred, no matter how well rationalized. It reveals the extent to which some persons of African descent have internalized the negations of African and African-American history and culture by persons of European descent.[12]

This is, of course, a critique of the extreme assimilationist position. Slightly more respectable versions of the position were held by Frederick Douglass and Booker T. Washington. Unlike Du Bois, whose theory of race couched in the language of "races have different messages" (at least in his 1897 essay) may be worked into a sort of politics of difference, Frederick Douglass and Booker T. Washington both couch the struggles for liberation (social, cultural, and political) in language that deemphasizes such things as race, nationality, and ethnicity while emphasizing African American membership in a universal humanity. But, as with the universalists among African philosophers, a similar weakness becomes evident. The assimilationist rush toward that inviting community called "humanity" turns out to be no less than a succumbing to a world defined by Europe. In their rush assimilationists fail to see that they pay the heavy price of uncritically accepting the prevailing dominant definitions of African American identity according to which Western conceptions of humanity become *the* conceptions of humanity. The move that subsumes African American identity too hastily into a universal humanity fails to adequately appreciate how the particularity of ethnic and cultural perspective is a crucial contribution to the development of an authentic philosophical pluralism. The warning here is about the hidden cost of an "integration" too hastily embraced.

African American experience has also exhibited an intermediate point between extreme assimilationist and pluralistic theories. That is the strategy of accommodation. Outlaw says of this strategy:

> The accommodationist's strategy is aimed at goals which involve aspects of assimilation, integration and nationalism. While any solutions to the problems of African people in America might involve each of these, nevertheless they must be employed with a critical understanding of their consequences, individually and conjointly, for our short and long-term development, and that of the country as a whole."[13]

Outlaw's warnings about minding the consequences of accommodation are well taken because failing to take heed exacts the same high toll of a hasty assimilationism. Of course there is much to recommend a struggle for liberation couched in the language of peaceful coexistence and all-around harmony. Yet such a struggle must remain aware of the disguises under which oppression perpetuates itself. An accommodation between unequals is tantamount to the assimilation of the weaker party.

Outlaw charts a third way—the way of a pluralist integration:

> The core of this orientation is a commitment to a politically, economically, and, in some ways, socially unified order composed of ethnically and racially diverse peoples, who maintain and perpetuate their distinctiveness to the extent that it does not threaten the unity of the whole (hence 'integration': the unification of diverse racial and ethnic groups into a mutually beneficial sociopolitical, economic order).[14]

Within African American experience the pluralist-integration orientation has manifested itself in various forms—especially as a racial solidarity and nationalism (cultural, economic, political). It must be remembered, however, that this is a pluralism that occurs in a thoroughly racist context. The institutions of the state itself, the social and cultural institutions, and the claims to a transcendental authority of a segment of the populace—all these have colluded to keep meaningful liberation from the group of African Americans. In this context an uncritical pluralism has consequences just as dangerous as assimilation, if not more so. This is the point made repeatedly by Du Bois. Assimilation would negate or make impossible the contribution of African Americans to the human community. It seems to escape Du Bois that a contribution is even more difficult to make in the oppressive environment in which one segment of the community has set itself up as objective judge of "valuable" contributions. The reader is invited here to recall the discussion about Senghor and negritude in Chapter 2. The Negro African who follows Senghor in deemphasizing any claims to reason while embracing emotion in a racist environment has sacrificed too much. She has acquiesced to be drawn into a Eurocentric framework that does not allow the possibility of other schemes of valuation. And even when other schemes of valuation are allowed they are considered fundamentally and conceptually lower in the order of preference from the standpoint of an objective (that is, a European) observer.

And so the struggle that has characterized African American experience and philosophy continues. It is a struggle to make a space in which African Americans strive to define themselves and to determine their own scheme of valuation. Yet there is a temptation that must be resisted—the temptation to set up this scheme as the single or final determination of inherent value. Experience should have taught us by now that conceptual frameworks differ from age to age, from culture to culture, and from epoch to epoch. The appropriate response to these particularities is not recourse to a relativism that asserts that each age, culture, or epoch should be judged only within its subjective contexts. Neither should the response be an essentialism that shuts off any real dialogue under the guise of universality. Africans and African Americans have much to learn from each other in their negotiations and struggles for liberation. They share a historical and transformative task of making real dialogue possible.

Connections with Feminism: Feminist Critiques of Western Philosophy

One of the aims of this discussion is to make a direct connection between the aims and methodologies of feminism and African philosophy. This is not a connection usually made either in theory or in practice. It is, however, important to find parallels between these practices that occupy different positions of marginality. A prominent feminist who has

made a direct connection between feminist and African struggles is Sandra Harding. In "The Curious Coincidence of Feminine and African
Moralities: Challenges for Feminist Theory," she argues that feminist
and African struggles are to be understood within the larger context of
difference (from the dominating class of white European males):

> We are different, not primarily by nature's design, but as a
> result of the social subjugations we have lived through and
> continue to experience. And yet, those histories of social sub-
> jugation offer a hope for the future. From those small differ-
> ences that we can now observe between the genders and
> among the races in different cultures can emerge a vast differ-
> ence between the defensively gendered and raced cultures
> we are, and the reciprocity-seeking, difference-appreciating,
> raceless and genderless cultures we could become. We could
> have cultural difference without the cultural domination en-
> demic to so much of the history of gender and race.[15]

Yet even as attempts are made to find these parallels in the situations
of feminists and Africans, philosophical analysis should be employed in
the direction of debunking the myth that they have been marginalized
in the same way. One problem Harding is particularly sensitive to is the
tendency to overlook differences (both within and between groups) in
this effort to highlight similar ontologies and epistemologies. By finding
parallels between discourses at the margins, the notion of "marginality"
is made problematic, and it becomes easier to delineate the different
spaces race, gender, and class occupy in the margins.

Contemporary feminist theory and practice aims to restore to women
the freedom, autonomy, and dignity that is due all persons. Feminists
have been successful in waging war against codified forms of legal and
economic discrimination as well as the more subtle variety of ways in
which women have been subordinated. Contemporary feminist Carol
Gould articulates the central concern of other feminists when she says:

> I think the preeminent value that ought to underlie the femi-
> nist movement is freedom, that is, self-development. This
> arises through the exercise of agency, that is, through the
> exercise of the human capacity for free choice, in forms of
> activity undertaken to realize one's purposes and to satisfy
> one's needs.[16]

Feminist theory does not arise in a vacuum. The value of freedom to exercise agency that Carol Gould and other feminists take as crucial is a challenge to classical approaches to philosophy that left out women or included them in very demeaning and disfiguring ways. Common to all classical approaches to philosophy is an acknowledgment of the nature of things, in particular reason and human nature. In the Western theory of ideas, however, reason and rationality have been presented as masculine, and the exclusion of women is evident in the language, religion, and social and political institutions. The classical outlook has as one of its foundations the notion of human nature as timeless in its essence. Classical philosophy also maintained the notion of reality as stable in its essence—firmly grounded in some unchanging truths. Feminists reject the purported stability of the classical outlook because attaining that stability rests on positing ineradicable differences between women and men. This tradition is oppressive because through its construction of difference women have been kept from independently willing and choosing their own projects. These radical projects, if carried through, would result in the complete unraveling of the categories of a classical philosophical tradition with its notions of a divinely ordered cosmos. The more moderate feminist projects aim to expand the philosophical tradition to be fully inclusive of women and to account for the commonalities between men and women in ways that do not overvalue one gender at the expense of the other.

Feminists make a broad range of critiques of Western philosophy. From a comparative standpoint, feminist critiques read very much like African critiques of Western philosophy. Here is a list of these feminist critiques for comparative purposes:

- Inordinately large numbers of philosophers are, and have been, (white) men.
- Because men and women bring different discursive resources to their understanding of their environments, there is a bias in the choice and definitions of problems when the process is filtered through masculine views of reason and rationality.
- There is a lack of concern for women's interests.
- The implicit assumption that the male represents the species leads to a bias in interpreting human experience.
- There is a neglect of "women's issues."
- There is a depreciation of "feminine" values.
- There is a denial of moral agency to women.

▣ There is a devaluation of women's moral experience.
▣ Radical feminist critiques question the very assumptions of objectivity and rationality that underlie Western philosophy.

Substituting "African" for "feminist" in these critiques does not change their relevance. Indeed, Susan Hegeman in "Speaking from the Margins" made the connection aptly:

▣ Clearly, the projects of feminism, various nationalisms, and movements centered around the liberation of racial, ethnic and/or class groups have many things in common. They frequently share concerns and face similar problems, and they are often based on similar (and mutually informed) conceptions of oppression and group identity. For example, most such movements of liberation describe their position in relation to dominant discourses as "marginal." Through this construction of difference, they attempt to describe a hierarchy of privilege, and hence of oppression, concept implicit in that of marginality.[17]

The similarities are striking. Feminists and African philosophers share certain features. Essentialist philosophy characterized women as beings who emphasized love, caring, and compassion over rationality. This was the same essentialist characterization of Africans as primitive, intuitive beings. There is now a shared rejection of the dominant traditions and a striving to bring about new perspectives; both are committed to examining the structures of power and its operations; both are suspicious of the categories in which the dominant traditions deal; and both seek to engage in practices whose intellectual tools do not deny agency arbitrarily to "others." It should not be surprising that feminists and African philosophers face similar dangers. Susan Hegeman has again noted:

The connection between some issues in feminism, and the debate about the existence of an African philosophy is striking because both feminists and African nationalists have at times embraced similar, essentialist, notions of alternatives for women and Africans respectively. In each case, these "marginal" rationalities are consciously opposed, respectively, to a perceived "masculine" or "European" rationality, both of which are described as seeing the world in terms of an opposition between the self and the other, the "I" and the "it."[18]

The ghost of essentialism here raises its head in feminist theory as well as in African philosophy. By not critically examining categories such as "woman" or "African," these deconstructive movements risk playing by the old rules of the dominant discourses. These old rules posited an essence, a persistent identity attached to the categories "woman," "African," and so on. Since these essences were static and immutable, essentialist models have been used against women, African, African Americans, and other groups at the margins. So these groups were seen as deficient in reason and rationality and thus could not partake fully in humanity. The caution here is that in the history of Western ideas, "different" has often meant "inferior." Contesting the mainstream equation of difference with inferiority is the challenge faced by feminists like Carol Gilligan. In her book *In a Different Voice: Psychological Theory and Women's Development*,[19] Gilligan provides empirical evidence for her feminist interpretation that rational thinking reflects masculine gender development in early childhood. Concentrating on applied ethics, Gilligan provides both empirical evidence and psychological analysis that strongly suggest that the lives of young boys and girls are constructed by social and historical conditions in ways that lead to a distinction between the male way of doing ethical theory and the female way. An example of these "different voices" is that boys grow up to emphasize reciprocity. Their ethical theories consequently focus on such concepts as equality, justice, rights, and objectivity. Girls, in comparison, grow up to stress responsiveness, and their ethical theories will therefore embody concepts such as care, love, trust, and compassion.

As noted already, the different voices of feminism have made valuable contributions to understanding the contradictions and inconsistencies of the dominant discourses. African women, however, sound the alarm against versions of Western feminism that are unwittingly imperial in their mission. The wave of feminism that can be traced to the progressive politics of the 1960s and 1970s in America (the politics driven by the civil rights movement) has appeared to African women an exclusive movement fighting for issues far removed from African realities. That wave of feminism is, often with good reason, perceived as representing the issues and interests of white, middle-class, heterosexual, Christian women. Problems creep in when representatives of this version of feminism assume that "black people are just like us." African women have not been alone in this perception of feminism. Elizabeth Spelman[20] has argued that a feminism that takes whiteness as paradigmatic results in, to use her phrase, "the erasure of black women." Feminism then acts in the same way as the masculinist theorizing to which it is a response. When Western feminism speaks from its experience as representative of the category "women," it forestalls the possibility of looking critically at the complexity of African societies and indeed the differences in the situations of white and black American women. Chief among the African complexities is, of course, the deep-seated patriarchy on the continent that does not allow what women do to be considered philosophical. There is an inherent bias in the very enterprise of defining African philosophy. In that patriarchal environment, additional burdens and restrictions fall on women. African women have long been engaged in writing that spans many genres—autobiography, short story, drama, and poetry.[21] Writers such as Buchi Emecheta, Flora Nwapa, Micere Mugo, Grace Ogot, Mariama Ba, and Bessie Head have dealt with themes that, had men dealt with them, would have been considered philosophical: themes such as modernity and the clash with local traditions, struggles against repression and racism in South Africa, and attempts to grapple with human concerns such as love and motherhood. These works do not feature in any discussions of African philosophy. One must suspect that the standards adopted for defining African philosophy are inherently biased. African women therefore call for an examination of the tradition within African philosophy that runs from Tempels, the "father" of African philosophy, to the modern professional philosophers. A sensitive feminism and a sensitivity to feminism can help in this effort.

Even as Western feminism gets more attuned to African realities, it would be dangerous to make too much of difference (either between white and black Americans or between Western and African women). Constructions of difference such as Gilligan's can be turned by antifeminists into devastating, if often inaccurate, criticisms. What Gilligan and other feminists value as a difference in emphasis arising from acculturation, the antifeminists pounce on as evidence of the rejection of reason. Antifeminists charge that by beginning with different assumptions about the nature of human personhood, feminists abandon the stability afforded by classical philosophy and its reliance on reason. Instead, feminist viewpoints are seen as trying to suppress or eliminate reason. The implication is that by focusing on care, love, trust, and compassion, feminists embrace the nonrational in a way that makes their work incapable of being judged by the usual criteria of clarity, comprehensiveness, and coherence. Feminists recognize these as false charges and implications without foundation—and accordingly they are suspicious of these manifestations of essentialism. To be sure, feminist approaches wish to transcend the traditional approaches to philosophy. They do not, however, want to achieve this by universalizing "feminine traits," for that would be to fall right back into the old essentialist trap. Alison Jaggar, a leading voice in contemporary feminism, captures this point all too well when she writes: "Invariably, anti-feminists have justified women's subordination in terms of perceived biological differences."[22] If feminists were to fall back on an invariant feminine essence or to exalt some chosen feminine trait as superior to male categories, that would be a recourse to the same biological differences posited by traditional approaches to philosophy.

African philosophers stand to gain by learning from the feminist retreat from the essential self. Here the comparativist will think about Senghor and the proponents of negritude. They perpetuate the subordination of Africans and the black people in the diaspora by clinging to notions of an invariant Negro African nature or essence. Feminist experience would immensely benefit the proponents of negritude because that experience has made clear that in the dominant frameworks of Western philosophy, "different" means "inferior."

Feminist theory and practice therefore share some common ground with African philosophy. There are ways in which their combined forces may benefit all these movements at the margins in their struggle to break into the dominant framework, its institutions, its language, and its culture.

Conclusion

African and African American philosophies and feminism have a convergence of interests, although their present practice does not reflect this truth. Each from its own particularity develops specific ways of organizing the production of knowledge, since each perspective brings different discursive resources to the understanding of our common world. Although their methodologies appear different, they grow more alike as we penetrate to an understanding of how they shape what can be known about human experience. As philosophical movements, they are engaged in a reevaluation of traditional philosophy that denied those at the margins equal opportunity to express their rationality and further denied them autonomy and agency.

Collectively, then, Africans, African Americans, and feminists are expanding the horizons and increasing the breadth of contemporary knowledge. Theoretically, though, much work needs to be done to integrate these perspectives in ways that will make clear that their aims and the bodies of knowledge they produce are complementary. To be sure, the interests of Africans are not served directly when feminists redefine economic productivity to include women's "traditional" activities like child rearing and home keeping. Nor are the interests of African Americans directly furthered by feminist challenges to the cultural biases of science. The convergence of interests is not always obvious. Indeed, it is not even clear that a mere recognition of the convergence will lead to an advancement of the shared interests. Yet as feminists radically question the category "woman" and Africans contest the category "African," the connection between them is that they are nontraditional intellectual approaches that are challenging the traditional ways of thinking in the established disciplines.

Study Questions

1. In what sense is African American social and political thought born out of struggle?

2. Distinguish carefully between the following coping strategies: accommodation and assimilation.

3. Are Leonard Harris and Lucius Outlaw suggesting different strategies for dealing with the African American predicament?

4. Do you think the charge that feminism has often resulted in the erasure of black women is a credible one?

5. Why are works by African women writers rarely discussed as African philosophy?

6. Discuss the specific ways in which the terms "margin" and "center" apply to (a) African philosophy, (b) African American philosophy, and (c) feminism.

7. Speculate on the kind of theoretical work you think is needed to forge and strengthen alliances among Africans, African Americans, and feminists.

Notes

1. William R. Jones, "The Legitimacy and Necessity of Black Philosophy: Some Preliminary Considerations," *The Philosophical Forum* 9, no. 2–3 (1977–78): 149–60.

2. Leonard Harris, ed., *Philosophy Born of Struggle: Anthology of Afro-American Philosophy from 1917* (Dubuque: Kendall/Hunt, 1983), ix.

3. Leonard Harris, "Philosophy Born of Struggle: Afro-American Philosophy since 1918," in *Philosophy and Cultures: Proceedings of the Second Afro-Asian Philosophy Conference, Nairobi, October/November 1981*, ed. Henry Odera Oruka and D. A. Masolo (Nairobi: Bookwise, 1983), 104.

4. Leonard Harris, " 'Believe It or Not' or The Ku Klux Klan and American

Philosophy Exposed," *APA Newsletter on Philosophy and the Black Experience* 95, no. 1 (Fall 1995): 6–8.

5. Harris, "Believe It or Not," 6.

6. Harris, "Believe It or Not," 7. On this point, Harris is mistaken. Howard University has been awarding M.A. degrees for at least a decade. It would be more accurate to say that currently no historically black colleges or universities offer doctoral degrees in philosophy.

7. Harris, "Believe It or Not," 7.

8. Harris, "Believe It or Not," 7.

9. John K. Mills, "Letter to the Editor," *Proceedings and Addresses of the APA* 69, no. 2 (1995): 123–4.

10. Harris, "Philosophy Born of Struggle," 99.

11. Lucius Outlaw, "African-American Philosophy: Social and Political Case Studies," *Social Science Information* 26, no. 1 (1987): 77–8.

12. Outlaw, "African-American Philosophy," 83.

13. Outlaw, "African-American Philosophy," 87.

14. Outlaw, "African-American Philosophy," 88.

15. Sandra Harding, "The Curious Coincidence of Feminine and African Moralities: Challenges for Feminist Theories," in *Women and Moral Theory*, ed. Eva Kittay and Diana Meyers (Savage, Md.: Rowman & Littlefield, 1987), 311–2.

16. Carol C. Gould, "Private Rights and Public Virtues: Women, the Family, and Democracy," in *Beyond Domination: New Perspectives on Women and Philosophy*, ed. Carol C. Gould (Totowa, N.J.: Rowman and Allanheld, 1983), 4.

17. Susan Hegeman, "Speaking from the Margins," *Sapina Newsletter: A Bulletin of the Society for African Philosophy in North America* 2, no. 2–3 (1989): 68.

18. Hegeman, "Speaking from the Margins," 72–3.

19. Carol Gilligan, *In a Different Voice: Psychological Theory and Women's Development* (Cambridge, Mass.: Harvard University Press, 1982).

20. Elizabeth Spelman, *Inessential Woman: Problems of Exclusion in Feminist Thought* (Boston: Beacon Press, 1988).

21. Some recent anthologies of note are Adeola James, *In Their Own Voices: African Women Writers Talk* (Portsmouth, N.H.: Heinemann, 1990); Stella and Frank Chipasula, eds., *The Heinemann Book of African Women's Poetry* (Portsmouth, N.H.: Heinemann, 1995); Charlotte Bruner, ed., *Unwinding Threads: Writings by Women in Africa* (Portsmouth, N.H.: Heinemann, 1994); Charlotte Bruner, ed., *The Heinemann Book of African Women's Writing* (Portsmouth, N.H.: Heinemann, 1993).

22. Alison Jaggar, "Human Biology in Feminist Theory: Sexual Equality Reconsidered," in *Beyond Domination: New Perspectives on Women and Philosophy*, ed. Carol C. Gould (Totowa, N.J.: Rowman and Allanheld, 1983), 21.

Conclusion

As we near the turn of the century, African philosophy is undergoing turns of its own. This is a unique opportunity to pause, take stock, and articulate with clarity and consistency the direction that will be taken in the future in light of what has gone before. Contemporary African philosophy must come to terms with its history and how that history helps or hinders the encounter with modernity. But because modernity is usually associated with science and Western thought systems, contemporary African intellectuals face what may be called the dilemma of modernity. The French critical theorist Jean Baudrillard aptly captures how this dilemma arises:

> Modernity is neither a sociological concept, nor a political concept, nor exactly a historical concept. It is a characteristic mode of civilization which opposes itself to tradition, that is to say, to all other anterior or traditional cultures: confronting the geographic and symbolic diversity of the latter, modernity imposes itself throughout the world as a homogeneous unity, irradiating from the Occident.[1]

Although modernity is desirable, for the African it has always seemed to be something of alien parentage to be understood only in reference to the Middle Ages, the Renaissance, the Industrial Revolution, and the cataclysmic changes of this century (changes, we may note, in which Africa's agency was minimal or nonexistent). Not only is it foreign, but modernity destroys the traditional cultures with which it comes in contact. Here is Baudrillard again: "As the canonical morality of change, it opposes itself to the canonical morality of tradition, but it is nevertheless just as wary of radical change."[2] Baudrillard's insight means that for African philosophy the dilemma is how to navigate between its own historical situatedness on the one hand, and on the other its project of decentering modernity in ways that make manifest a plurality of methods of knowledge production. This is the tension between a historical particularity and universalism. If African philosophers and intellectuals are to grapple successfully with the project of modernity, they must bring under suspicion all paradigms of knowledge production and organization that claim to be ahistorical and epistemologically transcendental. The challenge must be made without at the same time lapsing into the paralyzing postmodernist relativism whose clarion call is the incommensurability of discourses. To arrive at the position that the various ways of knowledge production are just so different that one way cannot be understood using the methods of another way is to lapse into the essentialism of, say, an Afrocentrist who responds to the skeptical questioner with "It's a black thing you just would not understand." The appropriate response to modernity would not be for African philosophy to replace Eurocentric visions of modernity with Afrocentric ones, but to proceed in a way that allows for transcultural and indeed transnational communication. African philosophy must be wary of repeating the mistakes of Europe. It is therefore imperative that African philosophers come face to face with their practice to root out features that may perpetuate the phase characterized by literature devoted to answering the question, Is there an African philosophy? The concern with identity was concurrent with a phase characterized by debate about what should count as a text and indeed on the intellectual merits of different texts. There are three lessons these phases hold for the future of the practice of African philosophy:

1. A meaningful practice will be wary of anachronism in interpretation, that is, the habit of throwing out as "confused" or "irrational" any views that do not fit the scheme of the interpreter.

2. It will avoid giving the false impression of inevitability, as if the thinkers taking part in these debates were a disciplined army marching toward the objective of "modern thought."

3. It will be careful about being betrayed by philosophical or other prejudices into an unjust and uncritical treatment of contending views.

The wave of the future will be for African philosophy to turn from the last thirty years' preoccupation with definition. Even more importantly, however, African philosophy will have to combine its substantive discussions with vigorous efforts to form alliances with African Americans and feminists who also have been denied or excluded from participation in the history of ideas. It is these connections that will situate

African philosophy in the broader context that offers exciting possibilities for the future of our practice.

Notes

1. Jean Baudrillard, "Modernity," *Canadian Journal of Political and Social Theory/Revue canadienne de théorie politique et sociale* 11, no. 3 (1987): 63–72.

2. Baudrillard, "Modernity," 63.

References

Articles

Appiah, Kwame Anthony. "African-American Philosophy?" *The Philosophical Forum* 24, no. 1–3 (1992–93): 11–34.

Baudrillard, Jean. "Modernity." *Canadian Journal of Political and Social Theory/ Revue canadienne de théorie politique et sociale* 11, no. 3 (1987): 63–72.

Bell, Richard H. "Narrative in African Philosophy." *Philosophy* 64 (1989): 363–79.

Bodunrin, Peter. "The Question of African Philosophy." *Philosophy* 56, no. 216 (April 1981): 167–79.

Cancel, Robert. "African-Language Literatures: Perspectives on Cultures and Identity." In *A History of Twentieth-Century African Literatures*, ed. Oyekan Owomoyela. Lincoln and London: University of Nebraska Press, 1993.

Du Bois, W. E. B. "The Conservation of Races." In *African Philosophy: Selected Readings*, ed. Albert Mosley. Englewood Cliffs, N.J.: Prentice Hall, 1995.

Echeruo, Michael J. C. "Negritude and History: Senghor's Argument with Frobenius." *Research in African Literatures* 24 (Winter 1993): 1–13.

English, Parker. "On Senghor's Theory of Negritude." In *African Philosophy: A Classical Approach*, ed. Parker English and Kibujjo M. Kalumba. Upper Saddle River, N.J.: Prentice Hall, 1996.

English, Parker, and Nancy Steele Hamme. "Using Art History and Philosophy to Compare a Traditional and a Contemporary Form of African Moral Thought." *Journal of Social Philosophy* 27, no. 2 (Fall 1996): 204–233.

Goody, J. "Review of Conversations with Ogotemmeli by M. Griaule." *American Anthropologist* 69, no. 2 (1967): 239–41.

Gould, Carol C. "Private Rights and Public Virtues: Women, the Family, and Democracy." In *Beyond Domination: New Perspectives on Women and Philosophy*, ed. Carol C. Gould. Totowa, N.J.: Rowman and Allanheld, 1983.

Harding, Sandra. "The Curious Coincidence of Feminine and African Moralities: Challenges for Feminist Theories." In *Women and Moral Theory*, ed. Eva Kittay and Diana Meyers. Savage, Md.: Rowman & Littlefield, 1987.

Harris, Leonard. "Philosophy Born of Struggle: Afro-American Philosophy since 1918." In *Philosophy and Cultures: Proceedings of the Second Afro-Asian Philosophy Conference, Nairobi, October/November, 1981*, ed. Henry Odera Oruka and D. A. Masolo. Nairobi: Bookwise, 1983.

———. " 'Believe It or Not' or The Ku Klux Klan and American Philosophy Exposed." *APA Newsletter on Philosophy and the Black Experience* 1 (Fall 1995): 6–8.

Hegeman, Susan. "Speaking from the Margins." *Sapina Newsletter: A Bulletin of the Society for African Philosophy in North America* 2, no. 2–3 (1989): 67–80.

Hountondji, Paulin. "Reason and Tradition." In *Philosophy and Cultures: Proceedings of the Second Afro-Asian Philosophy Conference, Nairobi, October/November 1981*, ed. Henry Odera Oruka and D. A. Masolo. Nairobi: Bookwise, 1983.

———. "The Pitfalls of Being Different." *Diogenes, International Council for Philosophy and Humanistic Studies* 131 (Fall 1985): 46–56.

———. "The Particular and the Universal." *Sapina Newsletter: A Bulletin of the Society for African Philosophy in North America* 2, no. 2–3 (1989): 1–66.

———. "African Philosophy: Myth and Reality." In *African Philosophy: The Essential Readings*, ed. Tsenay Serequeberhan. New York: Paragon House, 1991.

Irele, Abiola. "The African Imagination." *Research in African Literatures* 21 (Spring 1990): 49–67.

Jacques, T. Carlos. "Is There an African Philosophy? The Politics of a Question." *Sapina Newsletter: A Bulletin of the Society for African Philosophy in North America* 8, no. 1–2 (1995): 103–22.

Jaggar, Alison. "Human Biology in Feminist Theory: Sexual Equality Reconsidered." In *Beyond Domination: New Perspectives on Women and Philosophy*, ed. Carol C. Gould. Totowa, N.J.: Rowman and Allanheld, 1983.

Jones, William R. "The Legitimacy and Necessity of Black Philosophy: Some Preliminary Considerations." *The Philosophical Forum* 9, no. 2–3 (1977–78): 149–60.

Keita, Lansana. "The African Philosophical Tradition." In *African Philosophy: An Introduction*, ed. Richard Wright. Lanham, Md.: University Press of America, 1984.

———. "Contemporary African Philosophy: The Search for a Method." *Praxis International* 5, no. 2 (1985): 145–61.

Ki-Zerbo, Joseph. "La Personnalité Negro-Africaine." *Présence Africaine* 41 (1962): 137–43.

Maurier, Henri. "Do We Have an African Philosophy?" trans. Mildred M. McDevitt. In *African Philosophy: An Introduction*, ed. Richard A. Wright. Lanham, Md.: University Press of America, 1984.

Momoh, Campbell S. "African Philosophy: Does It Exist?" *Diogenes (International Council for Philosophy and Humanistic Studies)* 130 (Summer 1985): 73–104.

Odera Oruka, Henry. "Four Trends in Current African Philosophy." Paper presented at the conference on William Amo Symposium in Accra, Ghana (July 24–29, 1978).

———. "Sagacity in African Philosophy." In *African Philosophy: The Essential Readings*, ed. Tsenay Serequeberhan. New York: Paragon House, 1991.

Oduyoye, Mercy. "Reflections from a Third World Woman's Perspective: Women's Experience and Liberation Theologies." In *Irruption of the Third World: Challenge to Theology*, ed. Virginia Fabella and Sergio Torres. Maryknoll, N.Y.: Orbis Books, 1983.

Okolo, Okonda. "Tradition and Destiny: Horizons of an African Philosophical Hermeneutics." In *African Philosophy: The Essential Readings*, ed. Tsenay Serequeberhan. New York: Paragon House, 1991.

Onyewuenyi, Innocent C. "Is There an African Philosophy?" *Journal of African Studies* 3, no. 4 (1976–77): 513–28.

Outlaw, Lucius. "African Philosophy: Deconstructive and Reconstructive Challenges." In *Contemporary Philosophy: African Philosophy*, ed. Guttorm Floistad. Boston: Martinus Nijhoff, 1987.

———. "African-American Philosophy: Social and Political Case Studies." *Social Science Information* 26, no. 1 (1987): 75–97.

———. "Against the Grain of Modernity: The Politics of Difference and the Conservation of 'Race.' " *Man and World* 25 (1992): 443–68.

———. "African, African American, Africana Philosophy." *The Philosophical Forum* 24, no. 1–3 (1992–93): 63–93.

p'Bitek, Okot. "On Culture, Man and Freedom." In *Philosophy and Cultures: Proceedings of the Second Afro-Asian Philosophy Conference, October/November, 1981*, ed. Henry Odera Oruka and D.A. Masolo. Nairobi: Bookwise, 1983.

Ramodibe, Dorothy. "Women and Men Re-Creating Together the Church in Africa." *Voices from the Third World* 13, no. 2 (1990).

Senghor, Leopold Sédar. "Negritude and African Socialism." In *African Affairs*, No. 2, ed. Kenneth Kirkwood. London: Chatto and Windus, 1963.

Towa, Marcien. "Conditions for the Affirmation of a Modern Philosophical Thought." In *African Philosophy: The Essential Readings*, ed. Tsenay Serequeberhan. New York: Paragon House, 1991.

van Hook, Jay M. "Kenyan Sage Philosophy: A Review and Critique," *The Philosophical Forum* 27, no. 1 (1995): 54–65.

Wiredu, Kwasi. "Morality and Religion in Akan Thought." In *Philosophy and Cultures: Proceedings of the Second Afro-Asian Philosophy Conference, Nairobi, October/November 1981*, ed. Henry Odera Oruka and D. A. Masolo. Nairobi: Bookwise, 1983.

———. "On Defining African Philosophy." In *African Philosophy: The Essential Readings*, ed. Tsenay Serequeberhan. New York: Paragon House, 1991.

———. "African Philosophical Tradition: A Case Study of the Akan." *The Philosophical Forum* 24, no. 1–3 (1992–93): 35–62.

————. "The African Concept of Personhood." In *African-American Perspectives on Biomedical Ethics*, ed. Harley E. Flack and Edmund D. Pellegrino. Washington, D.C.: Georgetown University Press, 1992.

Zoe-Obianga, Rose. "The Role of Women in Present-Day Africa." In *African Theology En Route*, ed. K. Appiah-Kubi and Sergio Torres. Maryknoll, N.Y.: Orbis Books, 1979.

Books

Achebe, Chinua. *Morning Yet on Creation Day*. London: Heinemann, 1975.

————. *Anthills of the Savannah*. New York: Anchor Books, 1987.

————. *Arrow of God*. New York: Anchor Books, 1989.

————. *Things Fall Apart*. New York: Anchor Books, 1994.

Appiah, Kwame Anthony. *In My Father's House: Africa in the Philosophy of Culture*. New York: Oxford University Press, 1992.

Appiah, Kwame Anthony, and Amy Gutmann. *Color Conscious: The Political Morality of Race*. Princeton, N.J.: Princeton University Press, 1996.

Bernal, Martin. *Black Athena: The Afroasiatic Roots of Classical Civilization, Vol 1: The Fabrication of Ancient Greece 1785–1985*. New Brunswick, N.J.: Rutgers University Press, 1987.

Bruner, Charlotte, ed. *The Heinemann Book of African Women's Writing*. Portsmouth, N.H.: Heinemann, 1993.

————, ed. *Unwinding Threads: Writings by Women in Africa*. Portsmouth, N.H.: Heinemann, 1994.

Chipasula, Stella, and Frank Chipasula, eds. *The Heinemann Book of African Women's Poetry*. Portsmouth, N.H.: Heinemann, 1995.

Dillard, J. L. *Black English: Its History and Usage in the United States*. New York: Random House, 1972.

Diop, Cheikh Anta. *Nations negres et culture*. Paris: Présence Africaine, 1954.

————. *The African Origin of Civilization: Myth or Reality*, trans. Mercer Cook. Westport, Conn.: Lawrence Hill and Company, 1974.

————. *Precolonial Black Africa: A Comparative Study of the Political and Social Systems of Europe and Black Africa from Antiquity to the Formation of Modern States*, trans. Harold Salemson. Trenton, N.J.: Africa World Press Edition, 1987.

————. *Civilization or Barbarism: An Authentic Anthropology*, trans. Yaa-Lengi Meema Ngemi, ed. Harold J. Salemson and Marjolijn de Jager. Brooklyn: Lawrence Hill Books, 1991.

English, Parker, and Kibujjo M. Kalumba, eds. *African Philosophy: A Classical Approach*. Upper Saddle River, N.J.: Prentice Hall, 1996.

Eze, Emmanuel Chukwudi, ed. *African Philosophy: An Anthology*. Cambridge, Mass.: Blackwell, 1997.

————, ed. *Postcolonial African Philosophy: A Critical Reader*. Cambridge, Mass.: Blackwell, 1997.

————, ed. *Race and the Enlightenment: A Reader*. Cambridge, Mass.: Blackwell, 1997.

Fanon, Frantz. *Les Damnés de la Terre*. Paris: Présence Africaine, 1963, 1991.

Floistad, Guttorm, ed. *Contemporary Philosophy: African Philosophy*. Boston: Martinus Nijhoff, 1987.

Gilligan, Carol. *In a Different Voice: Psychological Theory and Women's Development*. Cambridge, Mass.: Harvard University Press, 1982.

Graness, Anke, and Kai Kresse, eds. *Sagacious Reasoning: Henry Odera Oruka in Memoriam*. Frankfurt: Peter Lang, 1997.

Greenberg, Joseph H. *The Languages of Africa*. Bloomington: Indiana University Press, 1966.

Griaule, Marcel. *Dieu d'Eau: entretiens avec Ogotemmeli*. Paris: Chene, 1948.

————. *Conversations with Ogotemmeli: An Introduction to Dogon Religious Ideas*. London: Oxford University Press, 1965.

Gyekye, Kwame. *An Essay on African Philosophical Thought: The Akan Conceptual Scheme*. Rev. ed. Philadelphia: Temple University Press, 1995.

Harris, Leonard, ed. *Philosophy Born of Struggle: Anthology of Afro-American Philosophy from 1917*. Dubuque: Kendall/Hunt, 1983.

Hountondji, Paulin. *African Philosophy: Myth and Reality*. Bloomington: Indiana University Press, 1983, 1996.

Jahn, Janheinz. *Muntu: An Outline of the New African Culture*. New York: Grove Press, 1961.

James, Adeola. *In Their Own Voices: African Women Writers Talk*. Portsmouth, N.H.: Heinemann, 1990.

Ki-Zerbo, Joseph, ed. *General History of Africa, Vol. 1: Methodology and African Prehistory*. Berkeley: University of California Press/UNESCO, 1981, 1990.

Klein, Thomas, Bruce Edwards, and Thomas Wymer, eds. *Great Ideas: Conversations Between Past and Present*. Fort Worth: Holt, Rinehart and Winston, 1991.

Knappert, Jan. *African Mythology: An Encyclopedia of Myth and Legend*. London: Diamond Books, 1995.

Kwame, Safro, ed. *Readings in African Philosophy: An Akan Collection*. New York: University Press of America, 1996.

Lefkowitz, Mary. *Not Out of Africa: How Afrocentrism Became an Excuse to Teach Myth as History*. New York: Basic Books, 1996.

Lefkowitz, Mary, and Guy MacLean Rogers, eds. *Black Athena Revisited*. Chapel Hill & London: University of North Carolina Press, 1996.

Levy-Bruhl, Lucien. *How Natives Think*. Princeton: Princeton University Press, 1986.

Makinde, M. Akin. *African Philosophy, Culture, and Traditional Medicine*. Athens: Ohio University Press, 1988.

Masolo, D. A. *African Philosophy in Search of Identity*. Bloomington: Indiana University Press, 1994.

Mazrui, Ali A., and Toby Kleban Levine, eds. *The Africans: A Reader.* New York: Praeger, 1986.

Mbiti, John S. *African Religions and Philosophy.* London: Heinemann, 1969.

Mosley, Albert G., ed. *African Philosophy: Selected Readings.* Englewood Cliffs, N.J.: Prentice Hall, 1995.

Mudimbe, V. Y. *The Invention of Africa: Gnosis, Philosophy, and the Order of Knowledge.* Bloomington: Indiana University Press, 1988.

Nkrumah, Kwame. *Consciencism.* New York: Monthly Review Press, 1970.

Odera Oruka, Henry, ed. *Sage Philosophy: Indigenous Thinkers and Modern Debate on African Philosophy,* Leiden: E. J. Brill, 1990.

Odera Oruka, Henry, and D. A. Masolo, eds. *Philosophy and Cultures: Proceedings of the Second Afro-Asian Philosophy Conference, Nairobi, October/November 1981.* Nairobi: Bookwise, 1983.

Okere, Theophilus. *"Can There Be an African Philosophy? A Hermeneutical Investigation with Special Reference to Igbo Culture."* Ph.D. diss., Louvain University, 1971.

Oleko, Nkombe. *"Métaphore et métonymie dans les symboles paremiologiques tetela."* Ph.D. diss., Louvain University, 1975.

Owomoyela, Oyekan, ed. *A History of Twentieth-Century African Literatures.* Lincoln and London: University of Nebraska Press, 1993.

Ricoeur, Paul. *Hermeneutics and the Social Sciences,* ed. and trans. John B. Thomson. Cambridge: Cambridge University Press, 1981.

Senghor, Leopold Sédar. *Liberté I: Negritude et humanisme.* Paris: Seuil, 1964.

———. *On African Socialism.* London: Pall Mall Press, 1964.

———. *Les Fondements de l'africanité ou negritude et arabité.* Paris: Présence Africaine, 1967.

Serequeberhan, Tsenay, ed. *African Philosophy: The Essential Readings.* New York: Paragon House, 1991.

———. *The Hermeneutics of African Philosophy: Horizon and Discourse.* New York: Routledge, 1994.

Soyinka, Wole. *Art, Dialogue, and Outrage.* New York: Pantheon, 1994.

Spelman, Elizabeth. *Inessential Woman: Problems of Exclusion in Feminist Thought.* Boston: Beacon Press, 1988.

Tempels, Placide. *Bantu Philosophy,* trans Rev. Colin King. Paris: Présence Africaine, 1959.

Thiong'o, Ngugi wa. *Barrel of a Pen: Resistance to Repression in Neo-Colonial Kenya.* Trenton, N.J.: Africa World Press, 1983.

———. *Decolonising the Mind: The Politics of Language in African Literature.* Portsmouth, N.H.: Heinemann, 1986.

———. *Moving the Centre: The Struggle for Cultural Freedoms.* Portsmouth, N.H.: Heinemann, 1993.

Towa, Marcien. *Essai sur la problematique philosophique dans l'Afrique actuelle.* Yaounde: Editions Clé, 1971.

Wiredu, Kwasi. *Philosophy and an African Culture*. Cambridge: Cambridge University Press, 1980.

———. *Cultural Universals and Particulars: An African Perspective*. Bloomington: Indiana University Press, 1996.

Wright, Richard, ed. *African Philosophy: An Introduction*. Lanham, Md.: University Press of America, 1984.

Index

About the Author

Samuel Oluoch Imbo is assistant professor of philosophy and the co-director of the African American Studies Program at Hamline University in St. Paul, Minnesota. He received his Ph.D. from Purdue University. He teaches and writes in the areas of comparative philosophy, African philosophy, and social and political philosophy.